THE

BUSINESS OF

CO-PARENTING

for Moms

**How to Be the CEO of Your
Divided Family
&
Live in Peace**

MERISSA V. GRAYSON, ESQ.

MVG Publishing c/o Merissa V. Grayson, 21151 S. Western Ave., Torrance, CA 90501

Ordering Information:
Quantity sales. Special discounts are available on quantity purchases by corporations, associations, and others. For details, contact the publisher at the address above.
Orders by U.S. trade bookstores and wholesalers. Please contact info@americasblendedfamilyexpert.com

Library of Congress Cataloging-in-Publication Data

Merissa V. Grayson, Esq.
The Business of Co-Parenting for Moms: How to Be the CEO of your Divided Family & Live in Peace
Edited by: Ebony Finley
Published By: MVG Publishing

Printed in the United States of America

Disclaimer: This book is intended only as an informative guide for those seeking tips for better co-parenting. This book is for informational purposes only and based on California law. The suggestions and strategies contained herein may not be suitable for your situation. You should consult with a professional therapist, coach, or attorney independently where appropriate, as neither the publisher nor the author will assume responsibility for any consequences of actions taken based upon the information herein. Although the author made efforts to provide quality information, the author does not make any promises, claims, or guarantees about the adequacy, or completeness of the information. As legal advice must be specifically tailored to the facts and circumstances of each case, the legal information contained herein is for informational purposes only and does not constitute legal advice. It is neither intended to create nor does create an attorney-client relationship. Should you need legal advice, you should consult with an attorney independently.

Dedication

For my mother, the epitome of certainty that children in divided families can flourish when endowed with immeasurable love, support, and persistence.

CONTENTS

PREFACE

Today, I am a Child Custody Attorney, Mediator, and Co-Parent Coach. I've been referred to as "America's Blended Family Expert" in part because of the work that I do in helping parents learn to co-parent successfully. But, it seems like just yesterday that my family fit the profile of a reality tv show. Move over "The Real Housewives" and "Love & Hip Hop."

I am a wife to an amazing man and a mother to three children who bring so much light to my world. One of my children is technically my stepson, whom I love as if he were my biological child. I've been his bonus mom eleven years now. I'd say we fit the profile of an "ideal" blended family. But, it hasn't always been this way. We've been through it all: fights, an intense custody battle, restraining orders, jail, police intervention, sadness, anger, frustrations, confusion and eventually understanding, appreciation, happiness... and *finally* peace. You might be reading this thinking that your situation is too far gone, and I remember feeling the same way. However, after years of trial and error, and learning some valuable lessons, our lives changed for the better and we created what feels like magic; two separate homes filled with harmony, peace and love.

Years later, when I opened my family law practice, I began to notice a recurring trend in the families I worked with. It seemed that even after my clients' legal issues were resolved, the struggle to co-parent cooperatively remained. Getting a legal "order" did nothing to change the day-to-day conflict or drama that their families faced. Their lives seemed to mirror the life I had prior to figuring out how to resolve my own co-parenting issues. So, I started working with my clients, sharing some of the strategies my family implemented and encouraging them to make a positive shift in the way they think and co-parent. As a result, many have achieved a level of peace that custody orders alone do not afford.

The Business of Co-Parenting series was inspired after looking back on my journey and realizing not only how drastically my family's life had changed for the better, but also the overwhelming positive changes in my clients' lives when we worked together to implement the same strategies that worked for my family. The series is 3-part. I was sure to include a title for Moms, Dads, and Stepparents, because I've found that the issues I help my clients work through are common based on their parental role.

This book was written for all moms who are struggling with either making the transition into a divided family or struggling with co-parenting peacefully with their child's father. Implementing some or all of the tips and practices mentioned in this book will help you not only resolve some of the problems you experience with your child's dad, but will also move you towards a life of peace. Now don't get me wrong. This book is not the cure-all to the problems every divided family will experience, but it was written with the most common problems in mind. Some things will apply to you, some things will not. Some things will work, some will not. Some things you will feel are common sense and some things will cause you to have an epiphany. One thing is certain, this book will challenge you to look at the full picture of your situation. At times, it will also challenge you to evaluate your own actions, your child's fathers' actions, and to consider all family members' feelings, perspectives, and expectations. At times, it will also challenge you to put your own emotions in check and make adjustments as necessary in order to foster a peaceful relationship between you and your child's father. It will guide you through different ways to co-parent peacefully if possible, or will also share alternative choices of action you can take if absolutely necessary. The key to gaining the most from this book is to be truthful with yourself. You have to face your *actual* reality, not the "reality" that you may have embedded into your mind that is not accurate. You have to be open-minded and willing to do the work. The level of peace our family gets to experience did not happen overnight. It took conscious effort and discipline.

Be forewarned, this book isn't for the faint of heart, as I am very direct and honest throughout - I do not sugarcoat the truth. However, you should know that it is all love, albeit "tough love." I have a genuine interest in minimizing the problems that many divided families face so that children will have a better future. So many divided families are struggling to co-parent peacefully and the majority of the time, it's because rather than looking at the full picture and seeking resolutions, both parties usually just play the blame game; accusing the other parent as being the reason their lives are filled with drama. Although your child's father could in-fact be the sole reason that the two of you are unable to co-parent, it is highly likely that you are also part of the problem and simply do not realize it. While true co-parenting requires both of you to work together, a significant factor that influences your situation is you. Unfortunately, you cannot control your child's father, but you can control your own actions and reactions. Perhaps you are doing all the correct things already; maybe you have done everything in your power to make your co-parenting situation the best it can possibly be, but maybe not.

You see, a large part of co-parenting effectively is based upon your mindset and how you handle situations as they arise. You have to learn to take control of the things that you can, and properly deal with the things you cannot control. Specifically, you must learn how to take control of your situation and recognize your responsibility, rather than impulsively blaming all of your problems on your child's father. This can be very hard to get used to, especially when your child's father has hurt you or otherwise caused problems in your life, but it's not impossible, and in fact it's very easy once you change your mindset and your actions. It is a concept I like to call <u>The Business of Co-Parenting</u>; commitment to learning and implementing this business will improve your situation drastically. It is my hope that by learning and implementing the strategies discussed in this book, your family won't have to go through what my family went through. But, if you're already going through it, it is also my hope that like my situation, your situation can drastically improve and you can experience the co-parenting peace you deserve.

It is my sincere hope that by writing this book and sharing the knowledge and wisdom that I have gained both through my own personal experience, as well as my professional experience, that I may serve as your guide to co-parenting effectively and living in peace.

Sincerely,

Merissa V. Grayson

INTRODUCTION

Statistics you should know:

Numerous studies have been conducted across decades on the effects living in a divided or blended family have on children. The unwavering consensus is – Children who live in divided or blended families face greater risks than their counterparts. Among other things, they are more likely to drop out of school, abuse drugs and alcohol, have greater and earlier sexual activity, experience incarceration and teenage pregnancy, and need psychological counseling.

But why? Why do children in divided/blended families face so many negative risks? It's not solely because their parents aren't together; there are several great children who come from divided/blended family homes. I believe that these risks are more likely to apply to children when their parents are on two separate pages, refuse to cooperate, and in essence, fail to protect the best interest of their children. I believe that with the right mindset and action, parents can ensure that their children evade these negative risks and thrive in spite of the fact that their parents live in two separate homes. So how do you accomplish this when you and the other parent are so far from the goal? By learning "The Business of Co-Parenting."

So, what exactly is **The Business of Co-Parenting**? I have discovered that the most effective way to manage your divided family and keep everyone and everything running smoothly is to manage it as if you were managing a business. Every well-established business has a Chief Executive Officer (CEO). The CEO is the highest-ranking person, in charge of total management and control of the business. Typically, the CEO's main responsibility is to act as a leader, director, and decision maker. That's where you come in. In order to master the business of co-parenting, you must become the CEO of your divided family. Using the tips in this book, as CEO, you will learn to take control of a negative or taxing co-parenting situation and redirect it into a markedly more positive direction. Equally important, you will learn to handle your co-parenting relationship with your child's father as a business relationship. By taking the business-approach as opposed to an emotional-approach you will clearly focus on the task at hand - to protect the most important asset of your business, your child. By treating your co-parenting relationship like a business, you will communicate clearly and directly, be proactive and minimize problems and the feelings of loss that your child may be experiencing. Consequently, when problems or disagreements arise - which unfortunately are oftentimes unavoidable - you will have the tools to effectively resolve or minimize them.

THE BUSINESS OF CO-PARENTING

I.

UNDERSTANDING THE DIVIDED RELATIONSHIP

In order to unlock the full potential of the business of co-parenting you must understand the divided relationship, be at peace within yourself, understand the dynamics of everyone else involved, how the circumstances affect them, and how to manage them accordingly

What happened?

What happened? At one point the two of you were a happy duo; either as a cute couple who were in love, dating to see if you were meant to be, or a fun fling who enjoyed each other for a season. Either way, at some point things were different; you spent time together and actually enjoyed it! Then something happened. The person who you were once so in love with, spent so much time with, had so much fun with, and enjoyed so much, became just the opposite. Now, you get irritated so easily with him, sometimes even for doing the things that used to make you smile: you hear his voice - you get annoyed, you see him - you get annoyed, he can't even breathe wrong without making you want to go off. Every time you have to think about him, you instantly get irritated and can't help but shake your head and wonder: "What the _____ (fill in the   blank

accordingly) was I thinking?" "How the _____ did I get into this mess?" And to put icing on the cake,

unlike when you first met, you now have a child with this person, so walking away and erasing him from your life is pretty much impossible. Your child either looks like him or has mannerisms that remind you of him that make you want to scream, throw something, crawl under a rock, or even change their DNA sometimes! Sound familiar? Don't worry, you're not alone. These are actually very natural feelings.

But why? Why did this happen? Out of all people, why did you have to be the one to become a single parent? The answer: because "Stuff Happens!" There's no such thing as a perfect life or relationship. People make mistakes, timing isn't always right, some people are afraid of commitment, some just don't want to commit, some don't want to be parents, some don't want to grow up yet, some didn't have positive role-models growing up, some need help, some are bitter, some are evil, some don't know how, some don't care. We ALL are humans...humans are flawed. You may be at fault for this happening, or you may not. And although at some point you will definitely need to address why this happened in order to lessen the chances of it happening in the future, your number one priority right now is not to dwell on what happened, who's at fault, or why it happened.

EVALUATE <u>YOUR</u> ACTIONS:

Where's your focus? Are you still stuck on figuring out what happened and/ or why you are in this position?

Oftentimes we find ourselves dwelling on the wrong things- things we cannot control. Doing this leads us nowhere. We end up stuck in a place we have no desire to be. It's important to remember that dwelling does not change a thing, action does. What's done is done, the past is the past. You don't have a time machine, you can't take back your relationship, and you definitely can't (and shouldn't want to) put your child back where he or she came from....what you can do is change what's going on right now.

ACTION STEP:

Your number one priority at this very moment is facing the facts and figuring out the "how":

How are you going to move past this relationship that didn't work?

How are you going to minimize and eventually terminate the drama and frustration that came with it?

How are you going to transform your strained relationship into a co-parenting relationship that works for the best interest of your family?

Divided + Blended Family Structure

❖ *Know Your Role: The CEO/Manager*

Years ago, my mother and I had a conversation about having children (this was way before I had children of my own). As she shared some stories about her life as a single mom, she said something that has stuck with me ever since. She said: "one thing I understood is that when you have a child, regardless of what the dad does, your child is your new responsibility." Although legally, child custody and support is not based upon the gender of the parents, generally, especially when children are young, the mother is the one that is assumed ultimately responsible for many things that occur in that child's life. Why is that? Part of it may be because you carried your child for more than nine months and maternity is undisputable. Paternity, on the other hand, can easily be disputed. Therefore, should your child's father decide to disappear into thin air, guess who is left? You! If your child's father <u>chooses</u> not to be involved in your child's life, guess who is left? You! Is this fair? No, but is it reality? Absolutely. This is evidenced by the disproportionate number of single moms compared to single dads. According to the U.S. Census Bureau, out of approximately 12 million single parent families in 2014, around 83% were headed by mothers.

Although in an ideal situation you would have your child's father there to share in all of the child-rearing responsibilities, the reality is that fathers and mothers think and operate differently. Most (not all) mothers assume the role of a mother by instinct and nature. It doesn't matter what stage a woman is at in her life, once she becomes a mother, she consciously and intentionally alters many aspects of her life, specifically her lifestyle and mindset, even before giving birth. Fathers, on the other hand, in many ways may continue the lifestyle they had before the baby came into the picture, waiting to make these shifts until after the child is born. Even then, there are still many things they still do that moms just can't - not the way they did pre-baby anyway. Many fathers don't assume the level of parental responsibility that mothers typically and automatically do, even in "traditional" families where the mom and dad are still together or married.

Trust me, it's not just you. If you were to survey all of the married (or even cohabiting couples with children you know) and ask them to describe each other's levels of parental responsibility, I'm certain the majority of them will admit that although the dads are involved and have some responsibilities, the mom is the caretaker and assumes the largest part of the parenting role. That's not necessarily a bad thing, it's just the way we naturally operate as a family unit. This is nothing new; it's been the tradition for ages.

But, for this reason, it's important that you understand your role as a mother, i.e., the CEO of your divided family. In a sense, you are in control of what happens with your family. You contribute to the type of relationship you build or do not build with your child's father. You have the potential to decrease the chances that your child will grow up fatherless, and will instead grow up with a thriving relationship with both parents; a part of one loving, yet divided family.

❖ *You are still a family:*

Yes, I said "family."

First and foremost, it's important to understand that although you and your child's father are no longer in a romantic or intimate relationship, you are still a family. I know, that may feel like an impossible feat right now, but it's your new reality. Your DNA chains have been joined to create your child who is a part of both of you. Whether you like it or not, you are eternally tied together, as your child now has family that stems from you and his or her father. They have grandparents, aunts, uncles, cousins, siblings, and possibly even nieces and/or nephews that you may not even know. You are now part of a divided family unit that must work together until your child reaches 18 years old, and perhaps beyond. So, why not do everything in your power to ensure that the next however many years you have left isn't full of unnecessary drama or stress, so that you can focus on what's most important – ensuring that your child can have the best life possible, despite the fact that you and their father aren't together.

Now, I know you are probably thinking: "How in the world am I supposed to consider myself to be a 'family' unit with someone I can't stand?" "I can hardly tolerate looking at or talking to him, how am I supposed to consider him family!?" Well, let me tell you, it's definitely a skill to be mastered, but it's not impossible. You must work hard at; it requires consistent dedication, understanding, compromise, and a level of maturity that many people are incapable of obtaining due to stubbornness, ignorance, or just plain old stupidity. But not you! You can tackle this, no problem. You will tackle this for your child. By reading this book you have taken a major step. You will master this "Business" of Co-Parenting. It's all about your mindset. And believe it or not, mastering this mindset is one of the best gifts you can give to your child.

❖   *Co-Parenting Explained:*

Co-parenting is a relationship between two parents who are not married, living together or otherwise in an intimate relationship, yet they work together with one another to organize their child's daily life and activities to ensure that the child receives the most consistent lifestyle and discipline possible and to ensure that each parent is fully aware of and involved in all issues related to their child. Essentially, the goal is to ensure that both parents and the child are all on the same page, and function as one family unit despite being divided into two separate homes. Sounds complicated right? It is! As I mentioned, it requires an unimaginable, inclined level of maturity. And chances are, there are some important things missing from your co-parenting arsenal that is preventing one or both of you from reaching that level.

It all starts with YOU

I know you are probably wondering: "How am I supposed to co-parent with someone who is not on the same page?" Well, that's the purpose of this book; to help YOU. It all starts with you.

Understanding the Divided Relationship

So here's the thing, despite your feelings towards your child's father, unless there is a legally established reason that your child should not have a relationship with their other parent, your child has a legal right to develop and maintain a loving, caring, stable relationship with both parents. Becoming a parent is a commitment that adults have to their children. This commitment has nothing to do with the relationship between the parents and should not be influenced by such. This is why maintaining a business model mindset is so important.

Even if your child's father isn't at that level yet, and seems far from there, your shift to this mindset can have a powerful impact. The changes you make alone can drastically improve your situation, as you'll be able to find peace within yourself, and hopefully encourage him to do the same. If not, then "it is what it is."- at least you will have the tools needed to ensure that you have done the best you can to encourage a co-parenting relationship, to remedy a lot of unnecessary problems and confusion, and to prepare you for a better single-parent lifestyle, cutting out all of the b.s., all for the best interest of your child.

The fact is: No matter how influential you are, you can't make people change, you can only change yourself.

People are who they are and no matter what, that's not going to change until THEY decide that change is necessary. BUT…you can influence others to want to change by being an example. It starts with you. If you want someone to do something, do a great job at showing them how it's done.

EVALUATE _YOUR_ ACTIONS:

Take a moment to examine your mindset:

- *Have you been treating your situation as though you are a divided family? Or as though your child's father is simply "your ex?"*

- *Do you consider him your "baby daddy?"*

- *Instead of taking control of your family and leading it like the CEO of a Fortune 500 company takes the lead, have you been waiting on him to take the lead and hoping things will fall into place?*

- *Have you ever stooped to his level and fueled unnecessary drama?*

ACTION STEP:

If you answered "yes" to any of these questions, your next action step is to take initiative to change the aura of your co-parenting relationship into that of a positive one. Your relationship with your child's father will not fix itself. In fact, it likely won't be fixed solely by any change of action on his behalf; to improve the quality of your co-parenting relationship, you must take the lead and you must be persistent. Otherwise you will be left waiting on the unknown for, who knows how long.

<u>Fighting Fires</u>

Have you ever heard the saying, "you can't fight fire with fire"? Well, that phrase isn't to be interpreted literally. After all, in actuality you can fight fire with fire; it's done by professionals all the time. Once, while watching the news, there was a huge story about an out of control fire that spread throughout one of the major Canyons in Southern California. The fire was spreading so rapidly due to high wind speeds that the standard methods normally used to put out fires were unsuccessful. So, specialists decided to use more advanced methods, including what they refer to as "back burning," a method of controlled burning. The idea of "back burning" is that by intentionally starting small fires along the main fire front, the small fires will burn back towards the large fire that is out of control and in essence, little flammable material will exist by the time the fire reaches the burnt area.

So what's the point? You can't successfully fight fire without specific skill and *intention*. It would never be wise to just go recklessly starting fires simply because another fire is out of control and expect to resolve the problem. The key to fighting a fire with fire is that in order to do so successfully, you must be a "professional," a "specialist." You must be tactful. This same principle should be applied in real life encounters with others, especially your child's other parent. If you don't like the way things are going, change what you can. The analogy to fire-fighting and co-parenting like a CEO is that, as a professional, reasonable parent, there will be times when changing your strategy is necessary in order to put out the fire you are dealing with.

For example, I once represented a man whose ex-wife obtained a restraining order against him by making false allegations of threats made against her. His first inclination was outrage and to call her, demanding that she tell the truth. This was obviously not the best approach because 1) there was a restraining order against him and 2) when dealing with someone who would lie to the court, especially to that extent, for their own benefit, every decision you make is critical and should be well thought out. Thankfully, he took the approach of a professional. Rather than acting on his initial feelings/emotions, he sought legal counsel, had the false charges dropped and subsequently obtained custody orders in his favor. Had he immediately jumped to contact her in his rage, his situation would've gotten worse before better. The key here is that he didn't stoop to her level, nor did he sit idly by and accept the false accusations without taking necessary and appropriate action. He fought fire with fire by acting as a professional co-parent, tactfully taking control of his situation. He tactfully started small fires which ultimately destroyed the one out of control. Similarly, the city couldn't stop the fire from spreading, so they changed their approach; they brought in a professional whose specialty is "back burning."

You must learn to be and think of yourself as a "professional" parent, whose specialty is the business of co-parenting for the best interest of your child, even in difficult situations. While you can't change his behavior or the fact that he is your child's dad, you can shift *your* mindset. Be the "back burner": Think about what YOU can do differently to influence change. If someone you are dealing with is combative and always wants to argue and fight, don't take part in it. Refuse to participate in any quarrels and let the person know how to reach you when they are done arguing with themselves. If you want to be respected, show respect. If you want consideration, show some consideration. And remember that change happens for others when THEY are ready. It's not going to happen overnight. But if you constantly greet someone who's combative with a generous smile (no matter how much you'd rather just tell them where to go – or worse), eventually they won't have a choice but to smile back. Anything else, they would simply appear psychotic for arguing with themselves.

I know this is extremely difficult, especially when people are on your last nerve, however, try to remember that you aren't doing this for *them*, you are doing it for your child and yourself. You have to deal with this person until your child turns 18 years old. Who better to be the professional that can control your situation than you? Now, don't get me wrong, even if you master the business of co-parenting, you will still face many obstacles, especially if the other parent refuses to be cooperative at all, but, by shifting your approach, you may be able to fight your fires with water. Or if necessary, tactfully and professionally with fire. So let's get started.

Dealing With Brokenness

Naturally, every girl (or at least almost every one) has a fairytale vision in her mind that one day she will meet the man of their dreams, have children, and live happily ever after as one big happy family. I know most of my friends growing up and I did! I always pictured myself dating the love of my life, who would one day ask for my hand in marriage; we'd have this huge wedding, and once we were set in our careers we'd have our first child together, our family would grow over the years (I wanted at least five kids) and live happily ever after. While it was a "cute" vision and I love the life I have now, the way things turned out were far from the sequence of a fairytale. Like many, I had no sense of reality or the fact that things rarely work out perfectly like the fairytales. There are so many things they forgot to tell us in those books, it's ridiculous! They forgot to mention that in real life, you will likely discover that the prince charming you think is your prince charming is probably not. They forgot to tell us that every relationship has its problems and that some relationships will not last forever. So, back to reality, when not only your relationship ends, but you also have a child from that relationship... what do you do next?

Naturally, one may think that when your relationship ends, the simple solution is to just get out, get away, walk away, and all of the problems will disappear. Unfortunately, it doesn't work like that. Marjorie Howard said it best when she said "in a blended family, everyone is broken." This is true in any divided family. If you think about it, there aren't too many people who would choose to have a child with someone and the relationship with that person not work out. Most people would not list "becoming a single parent" as one of their lifetime goals. And no child wants to grow up daddy-less, mother-less, or with separated parents. With that in mind, it's important to understand that when you and your child's father separated, your family dynamic essentially shifted into a place of brokenness and loss– lost relationships, lost friendships, lost love, lost trust, lost patience, lost pride, lost stability, lost peace, and so much more. With that territory often comes a lot of emotions, ill feelings, and even drama. So, what do you do to shift this dynamic? How are you going to ensure that you don't shift into a *lifetime* of drama?

The most important thing to understand about the emotions and ill feelings that you may be experiencing, is that for the best interest of you, your child, and your future, you must deal with them appropriately. What does "deal with them appropriately" mean? Well, it basically means that you need to figure out how to get over it! Whatever "it" is. Many parents come to me for help because they are experiencing so many difficulties that they blame on the other parent. However, after working with them, I realize that a lot of the current problems are caused by them. They are contributing to the problems that continue to manifest because they are still not over "it."

Now, before you assume I'm being insensitive, let me be clear, I'm not telling you that whatever feelings you have aren't justified or that dealing with them is going to be easy. In fact, your feelings probably are justified. However, you have a child whose interests are at stake, therefore, it is imperative that you face the fact that regardless of what happened in your relationship with him and how you currently feel about him, there is a bigger picture now. You have a child that you have to raise together. And getting over "it" is the first step to doing so successfully. This is the first step to ensuring that your child is the least negatively impacted by the division of your family, and that you will have a positive relationship with your child.

EVALUATE <u>YOUR</u> ACTIONS:

Take a moment to think about your feelings.

- *Are you still struggling with ill feelings towards your child's father?*

- *Do you still have feelings of anger, blame, hate, disappointment, betrayal, pain, sadness, or bitterness?*

- *Do you still have intimate feelings for him or a desire to be intimately involved with him that are interfering with your ability to move on? Rather than truly being "over it", are you still holding on?*

ACTION STEP:

If you answered "yes" to any of these questions, it's okay. After all, these feelings are a normal reaction to a relationship that didn't work out. What's not okay is holding onto these feelings without acknowledging them and trying to resolve them. Your next action step is to acknowledge that it's time to take control of your feelings and your mindset. If you find yourself struggling with these emotions, you should look into your intervention options. Keep in mind that a good CEO knows when to seek outside resources when the internal resources are not working.

Now is the time to take whatever steps are necessary to do what you need to do in order to finally be at peace with what happened, forgive your child's father, and completely let go and move on.

❖ *Breaking Ties/First Step to Peace*

He hurt you. While you thought the two of you were cool and on the same page, that wasn't the case. He lied, cheated, broke his promises, left you, or otherwise played you for the fool and as a result, you are hurting. You may feel disappointed, betrayed, sad, confused, embarrassed, or just straight up pissed off! You may wonder "what happened?" "Why would he do this?" "Who is this person?" You may even blame yourself at times, wondering, "how in the world did I not see this coming?" "What was I thinking?" Sometimes you think you'll be okay and just move on, other times you may question whether you'll ever be able to move on. Although you may outwardly be good at putting on a good front in order to fool everyone else into believing this doesn't faze you, deep down inside you may still be experiencing negative feelings toward him that you think may never go away.

If any of the above sounds familiar, don't worry, the feelings you are experiencing are normal! When you put your love and/or trust into someone and they turn around and betray you in a way you never imagined, having ill feelings for them is expected; to expect anything less would be unrealistic. The first step to overcoming these feelings is to be honest with yourself. In order to move on from pain, hurt, or other ill feelings toward someone, you must first acknowledge that there is a problem; acknowledge within yourself that you are still emotionally hindered from this situation. Although we as women claim, pretend to be, or maybe even believe that we are "okay" after being hurt by someone, the reality is that we are emotional creatures by nature who thrive off of our relationships with others.

<u>Getting "over it"</u>

If your feelings toward him are still ill, then you are not yet over it and you need to acknowledge that. Now let me be clear, you don't have to still *want* him, to remain captive to the emotional ties that must be severed in order to truly be over it. If you are still angry, sad, or hurt by whatever it is he did or did not do, you are not over it. To be over it you must not only forgive him for whatever happened, you must forgive yourself if you think you are at fault, and you must be willing and able to put the past behind you and let it go. If you do not work to truly get over it, you are in a sense letting his actions control your happiness, which will in turn affect your child's happiness.

Now, don't get me wrong. I'm not saying this is an easy task. It's much easier said than done. When you put your trust into someone and are hurt by that person, you can't help but hold onto those ill feelings, it's a natural human instinct. But for the best interest of your child, holding on to that illness is not an option because pain, anger, and other ill feelings tend to cloud your judgment and will make it virtually impossible to co-parent peacefully. So, how do you "get over it" once and for all? Well, the first thing you must understand is that it takes time. By no means will this happen overnight. However, I am a strong believer in one thing that may speed up the process, yet so many people are quick to decline - counseling. You may be thinking that you don't need counseling, and maybe you don't... but maybe you do.

Counseling

There are so many common misunderstandings and misconceptions about counseling. For some reason, so many people are caught up on the misguided idea that counseling is only for those who are "crazy," or those with a mental illness, depression, extreme grief, or those going through unimaginable, traumatizing events. No one wants to believe that their situation rises to the level of a need for counseling because of the negative connotations associated with it. Unfortunately, false perceptions about what counseling is, how it works, and who it's

24

designed for often keep those who will likely benefit from it the most from considering it for themselves.

Before you completely dismiss the idea of counseling, you should know that many people in a divided or blended family will need some counseling at some point, including your children; it's one of the many things that come with the territory needed to resolve the brokenness that divided and blended families experience. The fact is that counselors are professionals who assist people with many different aspects of life, not just those who are ready to jump over the edge. There are hundreds of types of counselors, each with their own specialty, serving their own chosen population. While it is true that some counselors do work with those who have severe mental illnesses, disorders, addictions, etc., there are numerous counselors across the globe who work with people dealing with everyday issues such as their careers, education, marriages, parenting, and health. Counseling can be a very good resource. It gives you a chance to talk over what is on your mind with a neutral person who can help you explore and understand the happenings in your life and teach you new skills and ways of looking at life so that you will be more capable of solving problems on your own. Whenever I get a new client, one of the first things I consider as part of their legal or coaching plan is counseling. Many of my clients are initially reluctant to enroll, but it never fails, those who follow the suggestion to at least give it a try, later admit that it was one of the best decisions they made and that it gave them great headway towards healing and progress. If you are still finding yourself struggling with any of the emotional aspects of your situation, this is definitely a solution you may want to consider. And, if your child is having difficulty with the transition to a divided family, blended family, or a new relationship with their father, you should definitely consider counseling for them.

Family Ties & Coaching/Co-Parent Classes

Counseling is not necessary in all situations that arise in divided families. If you consider yourself to be over what happened in the past, but still continue to struggle to effectively co-parent with your child's father due to high conflict or non-cooperation on his behalf, self-help books such as this one may suffice. However, if you need a little more hands-on guidance or help incorporating the principles in this book into your life, you may want to consider a co-parent coach. A co-parent coach is a professional who helps clients set and achieve personal goals. Their job is to help you identify and take tactful action toward goals for your divided/blended family. A coach will help enhance the things you are doing well and adjust the areas that are not working and which can be done better. In a sense, a co-parent coach can serve as a facilitator in helping you accomplish your full parenting potential despite your differences and difficulties with your child's father. Unlike counseling, the emphasis of coaching is not placed on what has happened in the past; coaching is geared towards your present thoughts and actions and how to shift them so it will positively impact your future.

The bottom line is, being a part of a divided family is not easy, especially for the parents. In fact, it's one of the most complicated things that you will have to do because there are so many different people involved, with so many different personalities, mindsets, and points of view. In order to unlock the potential of the business of co-parenting so that you can live in peace, you must understand the divided family and set a solid foundation; to do so you must not only be at peace within yourself, but you must also understand the dynamics of everyone else involved, how the circumstances affect them, how to manage them accordingly and hopefully instill peace into your divided family as a whole. In order to achieve this, you must deal with the past and set goals for the future. Again, the business of co-parenting is not something that comes naturally; it is a skill, a much defined one that will hopefully develop into a lifestyle.

II.

UNDERSTANDING
HIM

One of the key aspects to the business of co-parenting is understanding the type of father you are dealing with and his probable perspective on the overall divided family and his role in it.

Now, in no way am I indicating that you should always agree with his actions or even his perspective, but…by understanding, you can make informed decisions on how to manage your divided family more effectively based on your circumstances. Remember, you can't change someone else, but you can change the way you deal with them and lead by example. Here, I'm going to discuss what I believe are the most common categories of Fathers: 1) Absent Lover, Present Father; 2) The Erratic Dad; and 3) The Deadbeat. Whenever I work with my clients, their description of their children's dads include traits from one (and sometimes multiple) categories. The type of father he is will likely influence his perspective, his tendencies, and in turn the best way to interact with him. Either way, it's not going to be easy at first, but it is doable.

Absent Lover, Present Father

Also known as "the good dad," although you and your child's father are no longer intimately involved with each other, the absent lover, present father still has a genuine interest in being the best dad he can. If you are dealing with the absent lover, present father, you should consider yourself to be one of the luckiest moms on earth. I know that may be very hard to do because you don't always see eye to eye and you aren't "on the same page," however, children whose fathers are present in their lives have many advantages and face less risks than their counterparts. By your child's father being present in his or her life, that significantly minimizes the chance of your child falling into the category of one of the undesirable statistics. Now, don't get me wrong, he is far from perfect. Just like you, he makes mistakes and bad decisions from time to time, but all in all, he is a good dad; he wants to spend time with his children, love them, have fun with them, teach them, guide them, support them, provide for them, and be involved in almost every aspect of their lives. Believe it or not, there are millions of moms across the globe who would love to be in your position because the absent lover, present father has the potential to be the best dad to co-parent with; that is, if you fully understand and appreciate his role.

You see, the absent lover, present father only has one role - that of being a father. It doesn't matter how you feel about him, how he feels about you, or what happened in your relationship; that is no longer of concern. The only thing you should be concerned with at this point is how to develop a good relationship with him for co-parenting purposes only. It's totally possible that he still wants to make your relationship work, but for whatever reason that is not his top priority right now; he may have learned how to deal with the loss of the relationship so that he can move forward and focus solely on raising his child at this moment. It's also very possible that he's completely over your relationship, is tired of the "drama," or trying to make it work, and has moved on. Whatever the case is, none of that matters right now. His focus is on being present in his child's life on a consistent basis. This is great right!? Well, it can be.

That largely depends on you. You are the determining factor of whether this man can reach optimal parenting potential, have a good relationship with his child, and co-parent peacefully with you. Problems with him will likely arise if you are struggling with "letting it go", learning how to deal with the loss of the relationship, or understanding his perspective. If you are still holding on to those emotional ties or ill feelings, you could cause alienation between him and your child if you aren't careful. Over the last year, I've met so many distressed fathers who were not actively involved in their child's lives nearly as much as they wanted to be. Many of them complained that it was impossible to be involved because they constantly had to deal with drama; being faced with constant questions not related to the child, false accusations of abuse, threats to keep the child away, and in some instances just straight up degrading, disrespectful remarks from the child's mother. What's even more disturbing is that these fathers reported that a lot of these instances occurred in the presence of the children!

EVALUATE YOUR ACTIONS:

If you are experiencing difficulty co-parenting with an absent lover, present father:

- *Have you truly allowed him to be a father to your child without interfering?*

- *Have you put your personal feelings aside so they won't interfere with your judgment and his relationship with your child?*

- *Have you taken a moment to consider his feelings or his perspective?*

- *Have you sincerely tried co-parenting cooperatively with him?*

ACTION STEP:

If you answered "no" to any of these questions, there's a great chance that you are contributing to many of the problems that you are experiencing. It's likely he is genuinely trying to be a parent to your child; meanwhile you won't allow him to do that without unnecessary stress or drama. Your action step is to make a conscious effort to co-parent with your child's father. Take steps beyond those that you would normally take to level the parenting field.

I cannot stress enough the importance of putting

your child first when it comes to interacting with your child's father. Regardless of how you feel about your child's father, negative interaction with him is not good for your child, especially if done in his or her presence or within hearing distance. This is what I mean when I emphasize the importance of "getting over it." Although important to you, issues outside of those related to your child are not a part of co-parenting. If he doesn't want to be involved with you intimately, he doesn't have to. If he doesn't want to discuss your past relationship, he doesn't have to, and vice versa. His role as your child's father no longer has anything to do with your past relationship, but everything to do with your child. Yes, I understand that this is very frustrating and can leave you in an uncomfortable position, especially if you haven't gotten the closure you believe you are entitled to or participated in the counseling you may need. However, they have counseling and other programs and books to help you deal with that. It doesn't matter how uncomfortable you are, you still have an important goal that must be met for the best interest of your child - mastering the business of co-parenting so you can live in peace.

So how do you successfully co-parent with an

absent lover, present father? To start, the only way to begin to co-parent with this person peacefully is for YOU to get over "it," whether you have closure or not, so that you can think clearly and put your child's best interest first. This means that you must seek the necessary help needed to get over the past and set reachable goals for the future. Once you've done that, co-parenting with an absent lover, present father can actually be quite simple. All you have to do is let him do what he wants to do within reason...be a father. Allow and encourage him to develop a bond with his child. Give him the opportunity to spend time with your child without your interference. Start by thinking of him as your "business partner". Keep him informed of the happenings in your child's life and include him in the decision making processes as much as possible. Communicate with him regularly regarding your child and without forcing undesirable conversations on him that are unrelated to co-parenting, invite him to any events or programs your child is a part of, be cordial when you see him, and ensure that your child is aware that the two of you are working together as parents. The better relationship you have with him, the better relationship your child will have with him. (More ideas and tips are available in Chapter V.)

The Erratic Dad

Erratic dads are probably the most frustrating dads to co-parent with, but they may be the most common. Erratic dads are those unbalanced dads who love the *idea* of being a father, but are inconsistent. Many moms complain that he "parents at his convenience." Although he enjoys the time he spends with his children, he often forgets (or ignores) the fact that parenting is a full-time job, not just for you, but for him as well. He will take responsibility of your child if you ask him to, but seldom takes initiative. If he's not in the mood to parent, he'll place the burden on you. A lot of things related to your child may "conflict with his schedule." He will spend time with your child, but comes and goes as he pleases. He makes his own personal plans without considering who's going to take care of your child - assuming that you will. If it's not "his turn" to care for your child, you better believe he is living young, wild, and free. Sound familiar? If so, you're probably dealing with the erratic dad.

But don't worry! The good news is, although the erratic dad is inconsistent, with effort and guidance from you as his co-parent, it's likely he can make a smooth shift into that of a present father. It kind of goes back to the concept I discussed earlier, "motherly instinct." By nature, most (not all) mothers have natural parenting ability. Most of us don't have to be taught how to be mothers, it just happens. But, there are a few instances where even some mothers must be taught how to parent, and once they learn, many of them do a very good job. The same goes for many fathers, some of them must be shown how to be fathers. This is where our discussion (See Chapter I.) about leading by example comes in handy. You see, in most situations, the erratic dad isn't a *bad* dad. In fact, he's actually quite like the absent lover, present father, just not as *present*, at least not consistently. Unlike the present father, he needs a little more guidance in order to reach his full parenting potential. For whatever reason, he doesn't quite understand or appreciate much of the dynamics of parenting, especially co-parenting.

Factors such as whether his father was present in his life and what parenting patterns he witnessed as a child influence his parenting style and natural ability. Other factors are the type of crowd he hangs out with; whether his friends have children and are actively involved in their lives. If he has no examples, it's somewhat unrealistic to expect him to jump right into fatherhood and be successful, especially in a divided family. Think about it, back in the day, in many traditional families, mothers/wives were the caretakers and homemakers while the dads/husbands were the bread winners. If he grew up in this era, naturally, despite circumstances around him, he may have "inherited" these same parenting styles. He may not instinctively consider the fact that you work full-time, just like he does; he would have been accustomed to seeing mom handle all things child related and naturally expect you to do the same.

The key to having a positive, successful co-parenting relationship with the erratic dad is communication. Actually, communication is one of the key elements to all co-parenting relationships, but specifically to him; communicating about your expectations and limits is vital. With the erratic dad, you may have to sit down and have a discussion about what you need from him. Whether it be taking initiative to facilitate sports or extracurricular activities for your child, care for your child on specific days, or provide financial support to meet your child's needs, you must communicate the importance of his consistent contributions. If you have been handling all aspects of your child's daily life, he may have the perception that you don't need his help; he may assume that if you needed the help, you would ask. *Reality Check:* If you haven't been asking, but have just been getting frustrated by what he doesn't do or give, that's not his problem, it's yours. In fact, if you have been letting him parent this way without communicating these issues to him, you are part of the reason that he is this way, because you allow such behavior. Remember, you are the CEO of this divided family. If you want change to occur, you must do your part. At minimum, this requires communicating with him about your expectations and your child's needs. If you don't set clear expectations and boundaries, your child's dad may never shift from an erratic dad to a present one.

EVALUATE YOUR ACTIONS:

- *Have you communicated your co-parenting needs and expectations clearly to your child's father?*

- *Do you hold him accountable for parenting as agreed so that he must do his fair share?*

- *Do you make him pick up the pieces if and when he falls short of his parenting responsibilities?*

ACTION STEP:

If you answered "no" to either of these questions, your action step is to take the lead. Communicate your needs clearly so that there is no misunderstanding and hold him accountable for your child accordingly.

Now, let me be clear, regardless of how much communicating you do with an erratic dad, you must be mindful that consistency is new to him; he's used to either seeing or doing things erratically. We all know how things work when people are stuck in their ways - this is no different. The shift to a present father will not happen instantaneously. It may not even happen over a year. Truthfully, unless *he* wants to make the shift, it may never happen. Some people are how they are and will never change no matter the circumstances. If that's the case here, then you will have to handle that situation accordingly (see Chapter IV.) However, many erratic dads actually *want* to do more or are at least open to the idea. Similarly to the present father, you should make a conscious effort to allow and encourage the erratic dad to develop a bond with his child. Let him know that you appreciate his involvement and encourage him to do more. Invite him to events or programs your child is a part of. Keep him informed of the happenings in your child's life and include him in decision-making pertaining to your child.

To help facilitate and encourage this shift, you should start by delegating some of the co-parenting tasks. Start small; tell him the areas of parenting you can use his help in regularly and ask him what he is able to do. Remember, this is a team effort. That is why it's called *co*-parenting. Part of co-parenting is that you must show consideration when possible. By doing this, you put the ball in his court. If he's like most men, now that you have asked, he may try to take on everything. However, even if he's only able to do a little at first, at this point, something is better than what you've been getting right? Hopefully, as time goes on, he will eventually follow your lead and make a smooth transition into being present consistently. You may be surprised to learn that the erratic dad has wanted to be the present dad, only he either did not know how to or assumed you would not allow him to, especially if you have been the one to handle the majority of the parenting responsibilities. I've noticed that when you give him a chance, he will take it and his relationship with your children will continue to grow the more you encourage and support him in doing so.

One key to this transition is structure. Whatever parenting terms the two of you agree on; set schedules and deadlines, and stick to them. When it comes to his visitation, be firm at first. If it is his scheduled custodial day or week, insist that he adhere to his responsibilities. Make it his responsibility to ensure that your child is taken care of. If he needs help from you during his custodial time, require that he give you a minimum number of days' notice so that you can make arrangements accordingly. Help out when you can, but do not always inconvenience yourself at a moment's notice to take on his responsibility; if you are unable to make arrangements, hold him accountable. Patrice C. Washington said it best when she said "Sometimes, the only way to help people is to stop helping them."- this is very true. Sometimes we think we are helping people, and we are actually enabling them, giving them no incentive to do more or do better on their own. We learn habits by doing. The more he has to make appropriate arrangements for his child, the more it will become natural for him. Like you, he will begin to plan his week based upon days he does not have custody of your child. He will know that he can't just make arrangements for himself if he has not arranged for his child. This process may be overwhelming at first. After all, it requires you to put in a little more effort; it requires you to not only act as the CEO of your divided family, but also to step into the management position. As a Manager, you may have to *train* him to co-parent while also training yourself to be stern yet understanding, until he, like any other team member that a CEO has to manage, knows that you mean business. Your job may consist of creating schedules, writing tasks down for him, or even sending him reminders about what is going on in your child's life. With you leading, it is very possible to help him make the shift to a present father, and once he does, it will make the business of co-parenting a lot easier, and he will eventually be more like a parenting partner, participating in decision-making and collaborating with you more and more.

As mentioned, nothing will change overnight, it is definitely a process. In the meantime, it would be unrealistic and unfair to expect you to make endless efforts that do not ultimately result in positive change in your co-parenting relationship. Unfortunately, in some divided families the child's father is extremely unreasonable and uncooperative. Some people thrive off of drama and making others' lives difficult. If you have truly tried the things mentioned and rather than obtaining positive results, your child's father's actions consistently cause extreme disruptions and stress for you and your child, at some point you will reach your breaking point. If your child's father is in opposition to co-parenting peacefully, you may have no choice but to look to the family court system for resolutions, as he will likely remain an erratic dad indefinitely until he makes the decision to change. In the meantime, life must peacefully go on until that time comes; that is what the family court system is for; to make peace.

The Deadbeat

❖ *Deadbeat Defined*

Now let's talk about America's most prevalent and least favorite topic - the deadbeat dad. First, let me say, in my opinion, the term "deadbeat" is overused and misused. Whenever I hear someone call a parent a deadbeat, I usually ask: "What makes them a deadbeat?" The overwhelming response is always some variation of "because they don't have any money or pay child support." Huh? Is that it? Because they can't or don't pay you money, that makes them a deadbeat? Confused by this, I decided to look up the term 'deadbeat' to get a better understanding of the term. To my surprise, definitions I found were almost identical to the common responses I received. Most legal definitions of a "deadbeat" included references of a "parent who fails to pay child support."

Let me be clear, I understand that finances are important, however, considering the fact that being a parent requires much more important characteristics than "having money," I find this to be an absurd definition that is completely unfair because the definition is extremely broad and insensitive of specific circumstances. There are so many different circumstances that can lead to one's failure to pay child support. Specifically, and most commonly, Stuff Happens! Life is not perfect. Sometimes a parent may genuinely, temporarily be unable to afford to make substantial financial contributions to their child's life. With the way the economy fluctuates, even those with higher education and a lot of work experience have found themselves unemployed, underemployed, or otherwise struggling to make ends meet. Does this mean that parent should be labeled a "deadbeat" or not able to see their child because of their financial situation? Absolutely not! If that were the case, there would be a ridiculous increase in the amount of children who are parentless because financial problems affect both mothers and fathers. Automatically deeming one who does not pay child support (irrespective of specific circumstances, including any other contributions made to their child's life) a deadbeat is shallow and ridiculous.

Let's look at it another way, what about the dads who do contribute financially, but that is all they do? Is that enough? People tend to forget that it takes much more than money to raise a child. A man can pay all the money in the world in child support and still be a deadbeat. Society has us so wrapped up in riches and material things that we often disregard what is more important. Yes, it does take money to raise a child: children need food, clothing, shelter, and other necessaries of life. However, a child who has the necessaries of life, but does not have the time, attention, love and support they need from their parents is a lost child. Even if a parent is unable to provide financially, they should be able to contribute to their child's life in other aspects without being labeled as a deadbeat. There are plenty of parents who may be struggling financially, yet are phenomenal parents.

I believe that we should all re-define the word "deadbeat." My definition of a "deadbeat" is: one who *deliberately* fails to provide financial support for their child *and/or* refuses or fails to make reasonable efforts to be involved in their child's life as a parent.

EVALUATE YOUR ACTIONS:

If you are or have been referring to your child's father as a "deadbeat dad," take a moment to consider your reasoning for giving him this label. Is it because he truly is a deadbeat? Or is it because he doesn't pay you child support? If he doesn't pay, do you honestly believe that his failure to financially support your child is deliberate? Or is it possibly because he's having financial difficulty? If he's unable to provide financially, does he spend time with your child? Is he able to be involved in your child's life without interference from you? Or are you requiring that he <u>purchase</u> rights to be in your child's life (i.e. you will not allow him to be involved as a father unless he pays support)?

ACTION STEP:

Child Support and Custody/Visitation

Here's the thing, if you are not allowing your child's father to be involved in your child's life simply because he is not providing for him or her financially, I urge you to reconsider. So many moms make the mistake of thinking that because their child's father will not or is unable to pay child support, that he should not be allowed to see his child. **Big misconception – it doesn't really work that way**. Child support and child custody/visitation are two *separate and distinct* issues. Payment of support is not a prerequisite to parenting, that's why child support and government benefits were created; to compensate in situations where the child's support needs are not being adequately met. If he is not paying, there are remedies for that and there's a proper course of action that you should take in order to resolve that issue. However, willful failure to allow your child's father to spend time with his child could actually hurt you in the long run. This is especially true if you have court orders that provide for custody and visitation and you are not following them. Even if no orders exist, withholding your child from their father solely because he fails to pay child support can be detrimental.

Regardless of whether your child's father pays support or not, absent specific/dangerous circumstances, it is in your child's best interest to have a relationship with his or her father and to have frequent and continuing contact with him. Your interference with that will not only hinder your child's relationship with his or her father, but it could potentially cause your child to be bitter and damage *your* relationship with your child in the long run. To add insult to injury, your child's father may have a valid argument against you claiming that you do not make the best interest of your child a top priority and therefore are not the parent deserving primary custody.

Regardless of how you feel about his failure to pay support, you do not have the right to disregard your child's best interest because of your ill feelings. Your child does not know the difference between whether you receive child support or not and quite frankly, they don't really care. Typically, unless their parents sit them down and explain it to them, most children don't even know what child support is. A judge presiding over one of my cases once explained to the many parents in the courtroom that many children, in their independent mind frame (especially younger children), believe that the money is used to provide their wants and needs:

- Grows on trees

- Can be picked up at leisure from the bank

- Is unlimited on "those cards you swipe at the store."

- Flows freely out of money making machines (i.e. ATMs).

- Is unlimited as long as you go to work.

So although child support is often our top concern as parents, children could care less.

Over the years, I've interviewed numerous children in connection with my child custody law and mediation practice. When asked about their feelings and wishes, NOT ONE child responded that they wanted more child support from daddy. Similarly, not one wished daddy made more money or anything else related to money, except, I have had a few children request that their dad didn't have to work so much so they could spend more time with them. Out of all of my interviews, the only time the words "child support" were mentioned, was when one child said, "I wish mommy wasn't so mad at my dad about child support so that I can see him." What children consistently seem to care about the most when dad, child custody and or/support is at issue, is being able to spend time with their dad, and without worry. Children indeed need both money and quality time with both parents—one should not be at the mercy of the other.

Not only am I speaking from my professional experience, but I also speak from personal experience. During my childhood, my dad was not very active in my life; he was in the military and traveled a lot. He was constantly stationed across the country or in another country. We did not develop a true relationship until I became an adult. Although my father visited sometimes, called to speak to me on the phone regularly, and financially supported my mom in any way she needed (the two of them actually had a very positive co-parenting relationship), because he wasn't physically around on a regular basis, as I child, I felt as though there was a void.

Luckily, when I was eleven years old, my mom married my stepfather, who stepped right into the parenting role for me. My stepfather and I have a great relationship and I have since considered him to be my father; I never once wondered who would walk me down the aisle at my wedding. However, despite the close relationship that I have been blessed to have with my stepfather and how good of a dad he is to me, there has always been an inkling of resentment towards my biological father because of the minimal relationship I had with him. I often wondered why there was no effort to improve my personal relationship with him. As an adult, I now understand that my father's financial contributions to my mom helped tremendously when it came to providing for me. However, as a child, I did not understand or care about that; all I cared about was the fact that he wasn't around. What I remember most is that he didn't see any report cards or other accomplishments and that he wasn't present at sport events, band recitals, or other important moments. As a child I would've much rather had him as an active parent in my life than as a financial provider. If you can avoid this resentment for your child, by all means, you should.

The True Deadbeat

In contrast, if you are dealing with a true deadbeat, there are many things you must understand about him.

You Can't *Change Him...*

The most important thing to understand when dealing with a deadbeat dad is that you can't change him. As we discussed previously in Chapter I., people change when *they* are ready. Being a deadbeat is *not* natural. For most parents, once their child is born, it is natural to want to be a parent to that child regardless of the circumstances. Even those who "did not want" kids tend to become loving parents after the fact; they soon learn that it is no longer about what they want, but what's best for their child that now exists whether they wanted the child or not. Considering this, it's safe to say that unfortunately, if a person has entered into true "deadbeat" status, there is a great chance that he will remain there indefinitely.

Although in ideal situations a deadbeat will have a "change of heart," "find himself," or whatever else needs to happen for him to transform into that of an active parent, this may not happen. Just look at the vast number of fatherless children in our society today. With that being said, if this is where your child's father falls, life must go on, with or without him. You and your child do not have time to wait until he's *ready* and it would be unreasonable to expect you to. The good news is that when it comes to co-parenting, unfortunately and fortunately, the deadbeat is the easiest type of father to deal with because you don't really have to co-parent with him. True deadbeats are never (or hardly ever) around. The highest level of involvement (if any) that you will have from him in your life is that of paying child support as ordered. In many instances, you are able to maintain complete control of your child's life. The deadbeat does not care about making decisions related to your child, does not visit with your child, and your child may not even know he exists. The bad news is that regardless of what he does or doesn't do, you still have a child to take care of financially, physically, and emotionally.

If you are not very careful in how you deal with the deadbeat, he can be your family's worst nightmare, as he could potentially disrupt your family unit at any time. So what do you do? How do you ensure that your child does not suffer for lack of financial support? This is where that motherly instinct comes in handy. There is definitely not a "one size fits all" approach. You must think about things carefully and weigh your options depending on what you think is best for *your* family. Specifically, you must decide should he pay? Or should he go?

The Detrimental Child Support Chase

When dealing with the deadbeat who refuses to financially support your child, the most obvious remedy is to seek a court order for child support. But before you do this, you must consider the possible effects a child support order could have on your family. On one hand, a court order may be beneficial because if he is ordered to pay support and complies with the order, it will lessen your financial burden by whatever amount he contributes. On the other hand, it can be bad in the sense that pursuing this order can open up many doors of complication that you may not be prepared to deal with. If you do not carefully take the appropriate legal steps necessary to secure your parental rights and authority, you could later be faced with a very difficult and frustrating custody dispute should he all of a sudden decide that he wants to assume his parental role as a "father," solely for the purpose of reducing or terminating support.

As discussed, one is legally considered a deadbeat if he deliberately fails to pay court ordered child support. This definition does *not* encompass a father's failure to parent their child. So, legally speaking, despite one's absence from his child's life and failure to parent them, if he's paying his child support, he's not a "deadbeat" per se. By paying his child support, he has not legally "abandoned" his child, and therefore still maintains parental rights to that child. The problem with this is that in many situations, years down the line after the child has become accustomed to the people who are in his or her life and the lifestyle the mother has established, the father for one reason or another suddenly decides that he wants to be a parent. If this happens and you haven't taken the necessary legal steps (discussed in Chapter IV.) to prevent this, both you and your child's life can change drastically by now having to incorporate this new person into the picture. Not only could this be devastating for your child, but this could also be overwhelming for everyone and if not done carefully, can actually make matters worse rather than better.

For this reason, many moms decide to just let him go, without stressing the issue of support. This may be a good option for your family, or it may not, depending on your circumstances. I know, at first glance you may be thinking, "why on earth would I just let him off the hook; let him go without assuming responsibility for the life he helped me create?" The answer - to have a peaceful life! Many moms decide that they would just rather have peace for themselves and their families than fight a battle that will make their lives more complicated. If that peace comes with assuming full responsibility for the child as well, so be it! The key to determining if this is a reasonable option for your family is to determine why you are requesting child support. In a lot of these situations, where the moms ultimately decided to let him go, they admitted that they were not asking for support because they were really in *need* of it, but were asking for other reasons such as "to get back at him," "teach him a lesson," or "force him to be a father."

Both parents have a legal obligation to financially provide for their child until the child is no longer a minor. If you are seeking child support because you genuinely need the support, that is your right, it's completely understandable and is likely the best option for you. To lessen the chances of deadbeat dad disruption, be sure to read Chapter IV. of this book.

If you are able to financially provide for your child on your own, but want to "get back at" your child's father for not being responsible and/or to "teach him a lesson", do two things:

1) Read Chapter I., <u>Dealing with Division,</u> and Take Appropriate Action. Your continued ill feelings toward your child's father are likely to cause you more problems than you need;

2) Remember, it is not your job to teach him a lesson.

Your job is to be the CEO of your divided family and make decisions that will benefit you and your child. Although getting back at him may feel great for a moment, how is that going to help your situation? The reality is that a child support order is not going to "teach him a lesson." Unfortunately, any man who refuses to be a parent to his child is likely too far gone from reality to learn any lessons, especially from you. His issues run deep to the root of his soul, he has issues with himself that you do not have the capability to reach. The only thing your child support case is likely to do is piss him off. He probably will not pay the child support anyway, will begin a war of "getting back" at you and try to do everything he can to make your life miserable. Now, I'm in no way saying he should not be responsible for financially providing for his child - he absolutely should.

But, if you truly do not need the money you are seeking, you have to decide if it's worth it to begin and continue an ongoing battle with someone who will likely bring unnecessary stress into you and your child's lives.

Finally, many mothers make the mistake of thinking that by forcing (by way of a court order) a father to pay child support, that father will then be forced into fatherhood as well. **Just so you know, forcing someone who is not already involved in his child's life to pay child support will not force him into fatherhood.** You cannot force him to want to be a father, nor can you force him into your child's life. Truthfully, you should not want to. Why would you want to force someone who does not see the value of your child into your child's life? Children are precious and innocent. To have children is a blessing. To be a part of a child's life is a privilege; you must earn it consistently.

Every day, parents who do not work hard to maintain this privilege of parenthood have their children taken away from them. So ask yourself what makes him any different? What is he doing to earn the privilege of parenting your child? I completely understand the importance of having positive male role models and father figures in your child's life. However, more importantly I understand the effect of forcing a child into someone's life who does not really want them there in the first place - there is no benefit. Please be aware that many men who initially refuse to be a parent, but who are forced to contribute to a child financially, will later claim a desire to "spend more time" with their child. But know that in many cases, his desire to "spend more time" with your child has no reflection on his desire to be a parent. If that were the case, it would not have taken a child support order for him to do so. Often children become the victims of this deadbeat's plan to have his child support reduced.

Child Support Basics:

Generally, child support is determined by two major factors:

1) The income and certain expenses of the mother and the father, and

2) The amount of time the child spends with each parent.

Because the amount of time a deadbeat spends with his child is minimal, his child support amount is often higher than it would be if he was more involved in his child's life. So, what does he do? He begins to insist on being involved in your child's life more, so that as a result his child support amount may be reduced. In cases like these, his increased time would be a good thing if his intentions were genuine. However, because he still has the mentality of a deadbeat, this situation could become problematic for you and your family. Rather than force him into fatherhood, you in a sense may force your child into an unfair and uncomfortable situation. The deadbeat's actual time with your child will likely be minimal, as he will likely push your child off onto other people during his visitation time, he will make little to no efforts to assume any parental responsibility including being involved in your child's education, sports, or other activities, and he will not likely make any efforts to bond with your child in order to build a strong relationship with him or her. Your once consistent, peaceful home could possibly turn into a home of disarray and turmoil because you may spend much of your time trying to resolve several problems that this deadbeat has now caused.

Unfortunately, much of my job is spent trying to help families get out of these types of situations that could have been prevented. There was once a couple who had a son, and during the first six years of the son's life, the dad was completely absent by choice. In fact, for years, even after receiving positive paternity results, he denied that he was the father. The mom moved on with her life, and married someone else when their son was fairly young. The stepfather cared for this little boy as though he was his biological son, and this was the only father he had ever known.

Suddenly, after his sixth birthday; the biological father decided that he wanted to be his "father." His underlying motive was to lessen his court ordered child support amount. As a result, by the end of the custody and support proceedings, the father was granted visitation and his child support was reduced. Again, if his intentions were to spend more time with his child and build a relationship with him, this would be a good thing. But, unsurprisingly this was not his intention at all. He rarely shows up to his visitation and makes very little effort to bond with his son. Consequently, the child's accustomed schedule has been disrupted, he is having major adjustment problems, he is often confused and disappointed, and the entire family is now in need of counseling. In hindsight, the mother believes that had she not insisted on receiving child support (which she thought would "teach him a lesson"), her life would be less stressful and her family would be in a better place. I have seen this happen one too many times and it is something that can easily be prevented by taking appropriate precautions.

Signing Over Parental Rights

One of the most frequently asked questions received from parents relates to whether a parent can **sign over parental rights** to a child that they, for one reason or another, have no intention of assuming parental responsibility for. And while there is a widespread belief that a parent's desire to avoid parenthood is that simple- to just sign their rights over, the reality is that It's Not that simple!

But why not? Why can't a parent sign over parental rights if they don't want to be a parent? Well, there are several reasons:

1) The court's priority is to preserve the best interest of the child as much as possible.

Essentially, the courts don't want to leave a child fatherless (or motherless for that matter) on the impulse of one parent deciding that they no longer desire to be a parent. Thus, in order for a parent to avoid parental responsibility, special circumstances must be in place and certain procedures must be followed in order to protect the interests of the child.

In many states, the most practical way for a parent to sign over parental rights is through adoption. Adoption is available for both parents, or one (step-parent adoption) and allows the best of both worlds for the parent and the child; when a child is legally adopted, the parental ties with the biological parent(s) are severed, yet, the child is not left parentless because the adopting parents are stepping in.

Stepparent Adoption

If you have or plan to remarry and decide to "let him go," an additional option to consider is step-parent adoption. This option is only available to you if you and your partner are legally married (boyfriends don't count). Generally, to obtain a step-parent adoption, your child's biological father (the deadbeat) will have to give his consent. Since he does not have an interest in parenting and especially does not have an interest in financially supporting your child, you may be able to obtain his consent without dispute. After all, this is one of the only ways he can give up his parental rights and thereby be relieved of his financial obligation to support his child. If you discuss this option with him and he does not agree, don't worry, there's still hope. If a parent has abandoned his child (i.e., has deliberately been absent or failed to provide financial support), especially if it's been one year or more, the court can grant the step-parent adoption even if the deadbeat doesn't agree. The chances are even better in cases where the step-parent has stepped into the parenting role as your child's father, and has done so for an extended period of time. Whether the adoption will be granted is based upon what is in the best interest of your child. If you are dealing with a deadbeat, I'm certain you can make a pretty good argument that having a loving step-parent adopt your child in place of a deadbeat who does not want them anyway is in your child's best interest.

When Deadbeats Truly Change:

Sometimes, later on in life after years have been missed from your child's life, a "deadbeat" parent may finally decide to make an effort to change. He may contact you acknowledging his mistakes, his absence, and try to make things right with your child. Although later than ideal, this could be good for your child, as they have probably longed for a relationship with their dad, and if done right, their reunification may be successful. Here are a few things to keep in mind when facilitating their reunification.

Reunification counseling – If your child's father has been absent for a significant period of time and had no contact or very minimal contact with your child, there will likely be a lot of emotional issues that need to be addressed for the reunification to be successful. Qualified marriage and family therapists and other counselors offer counseling and other support services that lesson or otherwise resolve the upset and uncertainty that comes with the territory of having an absent father.

Supervised visits- Both you and your child may be uncomfortable with your child visiting with their father alone after long stretches of absence. When this is the case, supervised visits (requiring the presence of either a professional monitor, counselor, or trusted family member during visitation) will put you and your child at ease, while also allowing quality time with their father. This is a good way to start.

Step-up visitation plan- When children haven't seen their father for a long time, they may hit it off right after commencing or resuming their contact, or it may take a while. Until you see how things go, it's good to start things off slow to avoid unnecessary overwhelm. A step-up plan is essentially a visitation plan that builds up as time goes on. For example, you may start with 3 supervised visits and then graduate to 1 unsupervised day visit, and then multiple unsupervised daytime visits, and eventually progress to an overnight visit, and hopefully routine overnight weekends. How long each phase takes will really depend on your child and how he or she adjusts to their father; it could take weeks, months, or years. It's a good idea to put a plan in place, test it to see how things go, and adjust accordingly.

Domestic Violence & the Abusive Dad

The fact remains that unfortunately, at some point, many families experience domestic violence issues. Some families experience domestic violence and do not even realize it. Other families experience domestic violence continuously and do not know how or are afraid to get out of the situation. Whatever the case, having an abusive dad (or anyone for that matter) involved in you or your child's life can become a very dangerous situation. Just So You Know: Domestic Violence is broadly defined as a pattern of abusive behaviors by one or both partners in a domestic relationship.

Domestic Relationship:

A relationship is considered domestic if it is between family members, romantic partners, or the parents of a child. Abuse can be physical, economic, sexual, psychological, or emotional actions or threats of actions. This includes any behaviors that hurt, frighten, humiliate, intimidate, terrorize, manipulate, or blame someone. One is considered to have suffered from abuse if they have been a victim of physical aggression such as kicking, shoving, biting, hitting, restraining, slapping, throwing objects, or threats thereof. Abuse is not limited to physical actions. Sexual or emotional abuse, intimidation, neglect, controlling or domineering behavior, stalking, and even economic deprivation are also considered abuse.

You may be in an emotionally abusive relationship if your partner does not trust you and acts jealous or possessive, monitors your whereabouts at all times and tries to isolate you from friends and family, calls you names or continually criticizes you, punishes you by withholding affection, will not allow you to work, controls finances, refuses to share money, or punishes you by withholding money, or requires you to ask permission to do things. You may be in a sexually abusive relationship if your partner insults you in sexual ways, forces you into having sex or performing sexual acts, demanded sex while you were sick or after physically abusing you, involves other people in sexual activities with you, hurt you with weapons or other objects during sex, ignores your feelings about sex.

If one is a victim of domestic violence, they may seek future protection by filing an Application for a Domestic Violence Restraining Order. A Domestic Violence Restraining Order is basically a legal injunction that requires a party to do or not do certain acts. Orders to turn over firearms, not go within a certain distance of you, attend anger management/domestic violence classes, or classes to help recover from drug and alcohol abuse are just a few of the remedies that a restraining order may include. The length of the order and the scope of protection are determined by the court. One who refuses to comply with a domestic violence restraining order will face criminal or civil penalties and possibly, a prison sentence. Before one may file a request for a Domestic Violence Restraining Order, two requirements must be met:

1. There must be a domestic relationship; and
2. The filing party must have suffered abuse.

The bottom line is, if you or your child are or have been experiencing any of the behavior patterns mentioned above from anyone and have not reached the point where you are safe from harm (i.e., you are worried about your safety, walking on eggshells, or in fear of what's yet to come) it is important that you get help now! This book will not help you at this point because you have issues that are deeper than what is written here. Once you and your family are safe, you can pick up where you left off.

❖ *Co-Parenting after Domestic Violence*

If you've been a victim of domestic violence by your child's father, the idea of co-parenting with him is likely worrying. The good news is, children who are also victims of the domestic violence can also be protected by a restraining order. Even in situations where the children are not victims, if the court orders a restraining order against a parent, the restrained parent's rights to their children will be severely affected because as a result, most states presume that the perpetrator should not have custody of their child.

However, in situations where the children were not victims or if the father has otherwise overcome the presumption, the court may very well grant visitation (and sometimes even custody) to the perpetrator. If that happens, there is probably no sure way to guarantee that you'll be put at complete ease. However, there are several things you can do to protect yourself and your children from uncomfortable and traumatic interactions with their father, that will make it possible for you to co-parent without compromising your safety.

The most important things to do when co-parenting with your abuser is to establish boundaries. Boundaries are the lines that allow you to co-parent with your child's father, but also maintain you and your child's safety at the same time.

Custody/Visitation exchange location:

Where your custody and visitation exchanges take place definitely affects your comfort level and fear for your safety. There are several factors that may influence where you'll feel most comfortable exchanging your children, but here are a few examples of your options:

- *Curbside at home-* Depending on the age of your children, curbside exchanges may be a good option. These exchanges may be helpful because they allow you to stay with your routine and familiarity without actually having to interact with the other parent during the exchange. Essentially, during each exchange, the children walk, un-escorted between one parent's home and the other parent's vehicle. For example: At the end of dad's parenting time, he drives the kids to mom's house, stopping at the curb. Rather than walking the kids to the door, he simply lets the kids out of the car and watches them walk to mom's doorstep. Once he sees the children enter the home, he leaves…no drama, no interaction, just a visitation exchange.

- *Public place* – Public places are sometimes good for custody/visitation exchanges as well. Kid-friendly places such as Target, McDonald's or Walmart are in most cities and are good locations for exchanges. Not only are they filled with people, and brightly lit, but they also have cameras throughout the inner and outer store perimeters and provide receipts with date and time stamps on them, that will prove that a party showed up for the exchange. These exchanges are good because the kids won't feel like they're in the middle of conflict, but will rather feel as though their parents just chose a mutual spot to exchange them.

- *Police Station*- My least favorite, but oftentimes necessary exchange location option is the police station. This is the location of choice in cases with high conflict or when a fear of the other parent remains. While this location option provides the lighting, witnesses, and video surveillance that may come in handy if a dispute arises, this is the most intense place to exchange the children and they are sometimes left feeling like they're in the midst of a custody battle, embarrassed, and even, sad. The upside is that if something happens between the parents during the exchange, the police are literally steps away and can intervene and document incidents almost immediately.

Where your exchanges take place will depend on the severity of your domestic violence case, the current attitudes of you and the other parent and whether you're able to remain civil with each other, and whether you've overcome your fear of him.

Communication:

The parents will need to communicate somehow regarding the children. The best way to communicate with your abuser is to do so in writing. This will allow you to deliver your message, ask questions, etc. without having to actually sit down and speak with them. Both 'Talking Parents' and 'Our Family Wizard' (see details in Ch. 6) are good communication tools parents can use.

Phone contact with children:

When our children are away from us, we want to be able to get in contact with them. But how do you do that without interacting with their child's father?

-The best way to resolve this is to have designated phone contact time with your children for the parent who doesn't have custody on that day. The parents can then either have the children call the other parent at the designated time or have the parents call the children. Either way, the children will be the only ones to speak on the phone and the parents don't have to speak to each other at all. For example: Mom calls the kids on dad's phone, dad answers the phone call and hands the phone directly to the children without speaking with mom.

THE BUSINESS OF CO-PARENTING

III.

OUT WITH THE OLD, IN WITH THE NEW

So now that you and your child's father have separated, there are a lot of new adjustments that everyone in your divided family must make. It's important to put your personal feelings aside in order to make decisions that are in your child's best interest.

New schedule

An important aspect of co-parenting is establishing a schedule that will allow your child to spend time with you and his or her father. It is an established fact that it's in a child's best interest that he or she has frequent and continuing contact with both parents (absent extreme circumstances like abuse, neglect, etc.). When you're in a divided/blended family, it's important to develop as much consistency as possible for your children. Just as you and your family have a work schedule, school schedule, sports schedule, and extra-curricular activity schedule, it's important that you also establish a parenting schedule. To start, you will need to consider both of your schedules and your child's schedule (including school, tutoring, sports, extra-curricular activities, etc.) and determine who will be responsible for your child on which dates and times. Develop a schedule that works best for all of you, being sure to include your child's father as equally as possible. If your schedules allow, agree for him to pick your child up from school on certain days, take them to extracurricular activities, tutoring, do homework, etc. Remember, this is a co-parenting partnership, and should share the responsibilities and involvement as best as possible.

New Home Life

Making a transition into that of a divided family is especially difficult if you, your child, and his or her father previously lived together in the same home. First, you are faced with the task of figuring out if either of you will remain in your current home. If you decide to move out of the home, you are faced with the task of finding a new place to live. Even if you decide to stay in the home, the transition isn't necessarily easy because you have to adjust to your new home environment which previously consisted of two parents, but now only has one. Regardless, the transition is exactly that - a transition - and in order to make the process as smooth as possible, it is important that you maintain as much consistency as possible for the sake of your child.

If you move to a new home, try not to change school districts/schools if not absolutely necessary. At minimum, you should allow your child to continue established relationships with friends that remain in the area. Maintain as many of the same routines that were in place prior to the division and do not disrupt their extra-curricular activities by suddenly switching them to different teams, organizations, or clubs; the division of your family is enough change for now. The key here is not to avoid change, but to minimize additional and unnecessary change until your child has adjusted to this new, divided family situation. So many people make the mistake of deciding to completely uproot their lives because they need to "get away" so they can "start over."

Parents dealing with separation and their own feelings associated with the break up oftentimes overlook how this affects children involved. While family is obviously important to a child, so is the social life that the child has created for himself or herself. Making sudden moves like this in the midst of an already difficult transition can potentially be traumatizing for your child. Consider more than just your own feelings and think about how this will affect your child. While some children adjust quickly without issue, others must be guided through this process delicately. Remember, this is not their fault. Your child should not have to suffer simply because you and his or her father did not work out.

Blending Your Family

❖ *The New Woman*

If you were to see my ~~step~~son's mother and I together today, you'd see us cheering him on together at a sporting event, laughing, talking, and even holding or running after each other's kids. We talk and text all the time, wish each other happy birthday, send each other gifts on the holidays on behalf of our son, and support each other when needed. But it hasn't always been this way. I used to be "the new woman." For the longest, I couldn't understand why she wasn't as enthusiastic about me being in her son's life as I was. In hindsight, now I get it; she knew nothing about me. She had no idea that I was in this for the long haul and that I would love her son as my own.

Out of all of the new things a divided family must adjust to, most moms report the most difficult being the adjustment to new people in their child's life, specifically

- the new woman. To a certain extent, this is understandable. After all, this is your child we are talking about here and it's your duty as his or her mother to look out for his or her best interest. Considering the fact that this new woman is the equivalent of a stranger, reluctance is not unreasonable. As a mom, now I understand; just the thought of the wrong person entering into my children's lives makes me very uncomfortable. Besides, in this world we're living in, people can be crazy!

However, the reality is that since you and your child's father aren't together, it's going to happen at some point. Your child is going to meet the new woman; (in some cases, they'll meet more than one new woman, but that's a different book) you may like her, you may not. Unfortunately, regardless of whether you like her or not, if your child's father wants her to be involved in your child's life, then she will be; there's nothing you can or should want to do about it unless you have a very good reason. And no, "I don't want my child around another woman" is not a good reason. So unless you have a real good reason (i.e., she mistreats your child, is dangerous, literally crazy, etc.) it's time to step out of the girl zone and into the mature woman zone.

EVALUATE YOUR ACTIONS:

- *Do you refuse to accept your child's father's new woman and refuse to facilitate a relationship between her and your child?*

- *Do you insist that your child not be around the new woman?*

- *If you don't want your child around the new woman, what is your reason? Is it simply because you don't know her? Because she's not you?*

ACTION STEP:

If you answered "yes" to any of these questions, your next action step is to "woman up." It is time to face the fact that she is now going to be a part of your child's life and unless you can show that she is unfit to be around your child, there is nothing you can do about it.

<u>Become her friend</u>

How you handle the new woman will largely depend on whether you have the immature mindset of a girl, or the mature mindset of a woman. A mature woman, regardless of how she feels about her child's father moving on, will do what is necessary to make the best of the situation; in this case, ensuring that if another woman is going to be around her child, that it's the best relationship possible without interference caused by her. Although initially, it's natural to be apprehensive about another woman stepping into a parent-like role for your child, once you've properly dealt with the division between you and your child's father and any ill feelings you had toward him, you will be able to think and act maturely, making sure the sole focus is the best interest of your child regardless of what happened between you and their father and regardless of who is new in the picture. Believe it or not, the role this new woman plays in your child's life largely depends on your relationship with her (the new woman). Yes, you read right - I said **your relationship with her**.

When you or your child's father start seriously dating someone who will essentially be involved in your child's life, at that moment your divided family then becomes a *blended* family. This is especially true if either of you marry that person, which will technically make that person your child's step-parent. Even if neither of you actually get married, as long as there is another man or woman in the picture, the general principle is the same – this person's presence in your child's life can have a great impact, whether that be positive or negative. For this reason, it's important that you set aside whatever ill feelings you have toward your child's father or the new woman so that you can build a rapport with her. This goes back to the concept of being the CEO and *managing* the situation. You see, if this woman is going to be around your child, have influence over your child, it's important that you get to know her. Who exactly is she? What kind of family does she come from? What are her values and life goals? You may not think all of this matters, but it does…this is a person who will possibly be spending an enormous amount of time with your child, in your absence. You need not only to know that she has your child's best interest at heart, but she needs to know that *you* have your child's best interest at heart and that you'll do whatever is necessary to protect that, including setting your differences with her and/or your child's father aside so you can focus on co-parenting. To get to this point, you must eliminate as many negative vibes between the two of you as much as possible.

The better your relationship with her, the better her relationship with your child and theoretically, the better she will treat your child. The better she treats your child, the less drama you will have in your life, and the greater the chances you will have peace in your blended family. So how do you do this? Well, it's actually quite simple, through communication and by setting boundaries. As I have stated several times before, communication is key in divided families! Some boundaries will come naturally, others you will have to directly address and discuss. The first thing you need to consider is the fact that she is new to your family. She doesn't know you and you don't know her. She doesn't know if you are a "crazy baby mama" or a level-headed, mature mom. She doesn't know how you feel about a new woman being in the picture or how your child will respond to her presence.

SIDE NOTE: *Are you the "crazy baby mama?"* It's time to get real. Too many fathers refer to their child's mother as the "crazy baby mama." When I hear this term I automatically give the person who's being called crazy the benefit of the doubt. In most instances, it turns out that the accuser is usually over exaggerating or is the one who really displays "crazy" attributes. But there are some instances where the "crazy" label may not be so exaggerated. So, at this point, before we go any further, it's very important for you to evaluate your actions. *Do* you act like the "crazy" one? Are you extremely unreasonable when it comes to co-parenting? Do you constantly put your own interests before the interests of your child? Now that we have established that you are the new CEO of your divided/blended family, take a look at your behavior and determine if it is reasonable. The best way to understand how your actions affect others is to put yourself in that person's shoes. Be honest, logical and reasonable. Then answer the question, how would you react to "whatever" it is that you have done or said. If your reaction would be positive, then you've taken the correct approach. If your reaction would be negative or you would feel offended, then you've taken the incorrect approach. DO NOT be the "crazy baby mama." Understand that "crazy" attracts "crazy" and that equals *chaos!* Remember, you are the CEO. You don't have time for craziness or chaos. You are held to a higher standard that you must not only set but also maintain…..Now, back to "the other woman."

Although she may not show it, she may actually be

nervous coming into the situation because she doesn't know what to expect, and she won't know until you talk to her. A great way to break the ice with the new woman is to try to minimize these feelings that she may also be experiencing. Try to put her at ease and let her know that you are a mature woman whose only concern is that of your child. Let her know that you will not participate in or tolerate drama. Get to know her when she comes around. Ask about her family, where she grew up, what she does career-wise, etc. But whatever you do, please do not ask her questions about her relationship with your child's father; quite frankly, that's none of your business. Now, before you get your pen and paper and start writing your 20 questions, let me be clear, I'm not telling you to give her a pop quiz or drill her as if she's being interviewed. At this point an interview isn't necessary, as she already has the position of being a part of your child's life. Now that she's in this position, your goal is to figure out the best way to make her position work best for your family. Figure out her strengths and weaknesses and what she brings to the table. Spark a conversation with her similar to one that you would start with someone who you were introduced to by one of your close friends. The key is to be genuine. Almost everyone can smell the fake and the phony. You need to come off as being genuinely interested in getting to know her and you actually should be interested!

Offer to involve her in your child's activities if she has a genuine interest in being involved. This will not only give you an opportunity to see how she interacts with your child, but will also give you the opportunity to personally observe her personality as opposed to simply taking her word. Including her in your child's activities will also put your child at ease; he or she will be able to see the positive relationship and understand that it's ok for them to have the same positive relationship. On the other hand, this will also encourage your child to open up to you about this person, specifically if he or she has some reservations about her. The more your child sees that you are interested in building this relationship with the new woman, the more likely he or she will reveal whether they want that to happen. Whatever you do, under no circumstances should you reveal your ill feelings about the new woman to your child. This only leads to drama, confuses your child, and makes your child more uncomfortable than he or she may already be.

So what about those common cases where you

would ideally like to build a positive relationship with the new woman, but she is in fact the problem? What if she is full of drama, refuses to build a relationship with you, but would rather fight and overall just create a negative situation? Well, firstly, this all goes back to the goal of establishing a peaceful and cooperative relationship with your child's father. Once the two of you are on the same page, third party drama will dwindle down. Secondly, you have to think of her as an extension of your child's father and handle her the same way you would if he behaved in this manner (as discussed in Chapters I. and II.); by leading by example and fighting that fire with fire only if necessary. Remember, people cannot keep up drama with themselves, if they can that's when it's likely that they are crazy and need to seek professional help. The more reasonable you are, the more reasonable she will likely and eventually become. Although it may seem like *eventually* will never come, at some point, something has to give. Just continue to do the right thing, put your child's best interest first, and things will fall into place; if they don't you can easily take the *proper* steps necessary to get resolutions. Remember, you are the CEO, therefore you must handle things professionally, appropriately, and as necessary.

❖   *Your New Man*

So let's talk about your new man or your future new man. Your child's father isn't the only one who will bring someone new into the picture. You have a life too right? So at some point while you are establishing this new life, you will meet someone that you may be interested in. However, dating as a single mom is completely different than dating as a single dad. After the division, many dads begin dating again rather quickly. However, dads often date for themselves, for the fun of it, with little to no regard to the potential relationship the new woman may have with their children because much of the time, they do not intend to have a serious relationship with the new woman, at least not for a good while. They tend to date "behind the scenes." Since most dads spend significantly less time with their children than the mom does, they will usually date when it's not their custodial time. Dads usually do not bring their new woman into their child's life unless and until they decide to have a serious relationship with her, at which point she will become a part of your blended family, as discussed previously.

When it comes to single moms dating, I have found that there are commonly two different extremes.

On one hand, you have those who are reluctant to date, especially if the division is somewhat new. Many single moms believe they should not date; they make more time for their children, little to no time for dating or for themselves for that matter. They may not yet be ready or interested in dating again, or they may feel that it would be unfair to their child to yet again alter their lives by bringing in someone new. On the other hand, you have those who are quick to seek a new man in their lives for one reason or another. In some cases, it's simply because they are ready to move on with their lives and find something different than what they have had before. In other cases, it's because they do not feel *complete* without a significant other, and some are in search of a replacement father for their child.

Whatever the reason, one thing seems remarkably universal; when single moms finally decide to date, they date more so with the future in mind. They do not usually date just for the sake of dating, or solely to have fun. Moms tend to date with the thought of possibly and hopefully finding a significant other who can eventually be a father-figure for their child. If you too feel this way, don't worry, this is a natural feeling that accompanies that motherly instinct we discussed previously in Chapter I. Understand that dating again, when you are ready, is perfectly fine. Just ensure that you handle dating carefully with your children's interests in mind. Even if your child's father continues to be actively involved in your child's life, it is still important to understand that any man you bring into your child's life will play a significant role. Children watch and learn from everyone around them. For this reason, you must be very careful about who you allow to become an influence in your child's life. It's also important to remember that children need stability and consistency as much as possible. Your child's stability is already a little shaky because he or she now has two separate households; not to mention the other new factors in his or her life as mentioned before. So, when bringing new people into your child's life, it is important to be very mindful of what your child is already dealing with in order to minimize disorder. Specifically, take note of the following three very important points:

1) Every Man You Date Does Not Need to Meet Your Child

Prior to settling down with someone, you may go on several dates. Although many of these prospective mates may be good guys, that does not mean they should meet your child right away. Unfortunately, children do not understand the dating process. When they meet someone new, they will likely expect that person to become part of their life. That's great if you and the new guy hit it off and he takes on that role. But what if soon after your child meets this guy, you realize you are not feeling this guy? What if he turns out to be simply a thing of the moment? Having that person take part in your child's life early on, only to abruptly disappear can be detrimental to your child. Now when I say "meet," I don't mean if you happen to run into him while you and your child are out and about, turn the other way and take cover. I mean "meet" as in the guy becoming involved in your child's life.

Sometimes moms who are hopeful that a new guy they are dating will be "the one" quickly introduce their hopeful man to their child and start bringing him around on a consistent basis. Then, for one reason or another, she and the new man decide they aren't a good fit, and suddenly, he's gone. Although this may not be a big deal for most adults, this is huge for children! Especially if they have gotten to know this new man, look for him, and expect him to be around. In this situation, what results is a child who is now not only forced to adjust to a divided family, but also a new transition of having to adjust to the new man who has come and gone. If this happens more than once, you now are creating a cycle of people coming in and out of your child's life, which could ultimately influence his or her interaction with people in the future throughout his or her life; hence they may grow up to think this inconsistency is normal.

There are many people, both men and women, who grew up in environments where nothing was consistent, especially their relationships with those around them. This creates distrust and hinders their ability to build and maintain significant relationships with others. This vicious cycle is one that may or may not be broken depending on whether they get the professional help they need. You, however, can help prevent this cycle by simply being a little more careful about who you introduce into your child's life. Although there is no specific time limit in regards to how long you should be dating the new guy before you introduce him to your child, a good rule of thumb is that in order to meet your child, you and that person should be at the point where you are ready to take your dating relationship to the next level. Now, I'm not saying he has to "put a ring on it" before he can meet your child. But you should wait until the two of you decide to be in a committed relationship (i.e. "boyfriend/girlfriend") and that person must also be committed to accepting your child and plan to be there for the long haul as a parental figure. Of course this rule of thumb is not fool-proof, as things don't always work out as you expect, but it will potentially lessen the chances of unnecessary introductions and disappearances.

2) The New Man is Not Your "Friend" or Your Child's "Uncle"

If I hear of one more confused child referring to their mom's boyfriend as mommy's "friend" or "uncle so and so" I think I'm going to scream! Although referring to a guy you're dating as your "friend" may sound like a good idea, it's not! Calling this guy your "friend" does nothing but confuse your child, specifically by giving them a false perception of what a friend is. First of all, relationships with friends are platonic. Anything outside of that takes your relationship outside of the "friendship" zone. Next, in true friendships, *most* friendships last. Before classifying the guy you are dating as a "friend," ask yourself: "If for some reason this doesn't work out between us, will he

96

still be a part of my child's and my life?" If you can honestly answer this question "yes," then fine, refer to him as your friend. Conversely, if your answer is "no" or even "I don't know," he's *not* your friend, he is a guy you are dating. Remember, your child does not need any added confusion or inconsistency in his or her life. Creating this perception that "friends" come and go is contributing to the creation of the in and out cycle previously discussed and is not in your child's best interest.

The same principle applies to having your child call the guy you are dating "uncle"…what!? This is not your brother (is it?). Nor is this your close friend that you consider the brother you never had! Stop it! Again, this is just confusing your child. *(Side note: I'm very saddened by the fact that I have to include this paragraph in this book, but I have seen and heard enough).* Since when did it become okay to date your brother?… Never! And I would hope that you do not want to lead your child to believe this. He's not your brother, he's not your child's uncle so please, do not refer to him as such.

3) You and The New Man Must Know and Understand His Role and Boundaries

With the exception of situations where your child's father is a true deadbeat, the new man's role is not to replace your child's dad. However, he should be ready, willing, and able to assume a positive father-figure role in your child's life based on the relationship that he has with you. He should also understand and respect the fact that your child has a dad, and act accordingly. Under no circumstances should you direct your child to refer to the new man as "dad," "daddy" or any variation of that title; this is the ultimate sign of disrespect to his or her father and can cause a lot of major problems. You tell me, do you want your child calling the new woman "mommy?" I'm guessing not.

You must consider that just as women are apprehensive about new women coming into their children's lives, so are men about new men coming into their children's lives; rightfully so. So what do you do? The best approach to take when bringing a new man into your divided family is to show your child's father the same respect that you would like him to show you. I know I may sound repetitive when I say, "lead by example," but doing so facilitates the greatest potential for a positive relationship with your child's father in most situations. Consider how this new man coming into the picture would make your child's father feel and try to minimize the reluctance he may have for this change by being respectful to the relationship that he has with your child and that once existed between the two of you.

Prior to introducing your new man to your child, talk to your child's father about it. Let him know that you have been dating someone and that you are now at a serious place in your relationship which includes introducing him to your child. Explain that out of respect for him and in consideration of your child's best interest, you wanted to wait until you knew this person was in it for the long haul and wasn't just a thing for the moment. Ask him if he would like to meet the new man first, before you introduce him to your child. He may say yes, he may decline, but by putting the ball in his court and giving him the option, he will see that you are consciously making an effort to co-parent with him and make sure he's aware of and may be involved in major decisions that will essentially affect your child. I know this seems like a lot, but it's a very important part of the business of co-parenting.

Even if your child's father did not show you the same courtesy that I am advising you to show him, remember, always lead by example. Show him the right way to co-parent and hopefully he will eventually follow. One of the key characteristics of a good co-parent is the ability to be the bigger person no matter what the other parent does. Do not expect him to lead your divided family. You must be the CEO and be proactive! You want to neutralize as many potentially negative situations as possible. By communicating your intentions to your child's father beforehand, you are starting off on a more positive note than you would if you were to all of a sudden have some new guy around your child without notice and your child's father found out from a third party, or worse - your child. This also helps reassure your child's father that you are not trying to replace him as your child's father and may even encourage him to take the lead in getting to know your new man and incorporating him into your divided/blended family.

IV.

THE LEGAL WAY

Apart from your divided family situation, in order to protect your family from unnecessary interruptions and prevent unnecessary problems, the most important thing you need to do is take certain legal actions.

One of the most beneficial things you can do for your divided family is establish child custody orders. Formal custody orders make divided/blended family life a little less complicated. Not only will it create a legal record as to who has the authority to make decisions related to your child, but it will also outline who your child will live with, what the other parent's visitation will be (if any), and much more. Many families make the mistake of skipping this step because they don't realize the consequences of not having orders. It's important to know that despite what you may believe is the best custody/visitation arrangement for your children, unless you and the other parent agree on these arrangements, custody is not automatic.

When a child's parents are unmarried, unless a court action already exists related to custody/guardianship of your child, parents "technically" don't have any legal/enforceable rights to that child. In order to establish these rights, a court action establishing parentage must be filed-this must be done even if the parents both signed the child's birth certificate or voluntary declaration of paternity. Even when a child's parents are married, custody is still not simple. When parents separate or divorce, neither parent is any more entitled to custody of the children than the other until the court makes orders. Because custody is essentially a "free for all" before the court makes orders (either parent may keep the children with them, pick them up from school, etc.) many families end up fighting over the kids unnecessarily, causing disruption in daily routines and preventing stability for the children involved. For this reason, it's important to request specific custody orders simultaneously when filing for divorce or as soon as possible thereafter.

By establishing custody early on, your child's status quo is documented for the record in case there is a custody dispute later. There will be no question as to who has rights to your child and any violations of those rights are easily enforceable.

Steps to establish custody orders

Thanks to television and media, many families think that the only way to establish custody orders is to "go to court." Going to court is one way for you to establish custody orders, but in many cases it's unnecessary. Letting a judge decide the fate of your divided/blended family rarely fares well for anyone involved. Although on television, the court process is often portrayed as being easy breezy, in reality, it's much more complex. When representing clients, I try my best to avoid the courtroom as much as possible. In my opinion, this should be a last resort.

FAQ: If me and my child's father agree to work together regarding custody do I still need custody orders?

If your child's father is present, custody orders will establish stability and parenting guidelines that will help minimize future confusion. When parents are civil enough to cooperate, they assume they can just "work it out" between themselves without the need for any formal arrangements such as a custody order or written parenting plan.

My answer to this question is almost always, you don't have to, but you should.

I know you may think that formalizing your agreement is an unnecessary step, and, there is a very slim chance that you are right. Yes, the idea of working together, taking things day by day, and caring for the kids according to what's going on with your family's daily schedule is a great idea. But, more often than not, these informal arrangements become problematic. This is especially true when the parents first separate or before they have consciously established a positive co-parenting relationship. If you fail to formalize your agreement, you are very possibly setting yourself up for unnecessary chaos.

If you and your child's father get along well, great! However, it is to be expected that you will not always get along and you definitely will not agree on everything. Heck, if you did agree on everything you would probably still be together, right? In divided/blended families, at some point, parents typically will likely have a disagreement regarding the children's schedule, activities, childcare, financial needs, discipline, or other issues; if there is no set remedy in place, that's when the drama begins. When this happens, one parent will refuse to cooperate, refuse:

- to "allow" the kids to go with the other parent,

- to contribute to a financial obligation,

- to confer with the other parent regarding an important

decision related to the kids,

the list goes on and on of the problems that can potentially arise when informal arrangements go sour.

The safest approach to protect your family is to be proactive, understanding the potential for problems and disagreements, and plan accordingly. Hopefully, you can develop a cooperative co-parenting relationship and live happily ever after, but…you know the saying "prepare for the worst, hope for the best." That is especially true here. The best way to prepare for the worst is to establish a formal parenting plan. Essentially, this means you want to establish a parenting plan and then have it signed by a judge so that it becomes an enforceable court order, albeit one that YOU create, it will still be enforceable in the event that you or the other parent wake up one day or randomly have a change of heart and decide that you aren't going to follow the agreement.

Remember, co-parenting is a business and the only asset of your business is your child. Your job is to take preventative steps that are necessary to protect your child. All successful businesses have written agreements that govern their business relationships; those that do not are usually the ones that do not take their business seriously and have the most legal problems in the long run. Similarly, co-parents who do not have formalized agreements are the ones who generally end up seeking emergency court orders and/or fighting in ugly custody battles. The purpose of formalizing your parenting schedule is to protect you and your children from unnecessary spontaneous disputes, thereby maintaining peace.

The idea is that by formalizing your agreement you will both be held accountable for your actions. You will have more of an incentive to follow the agreement, because you will know that failure to do so can result in criminal penalties. Additionally, you will feel secure in knowing that in the event that the other parent does violate the order, you have the option to seek enforcement from the police or court system if absolutely necessary. I have lost count of the number of situations that I have handled that included complaints of their child being "kidnapped" by the other parent. The most common situations are those where the parents have been alternating custody of their child on their own, without a court order.

Keep in mind, circumstances surrounding your family will change constantly and you may need to deviate from your written parenting plan accordingly. You will always have the option to agree to change things day by day if necessary. But, once your plan is signed by the court, even if you never have to take action to enforce it, your family will have the security in knowing that there are rules, schedules, and guidelines in place that are best for your family, irrespective of how you may be feeling about each other in a particular moment, that must be followed to maintain stability and consistency for your children. If your child's father is present, formal orders will provide specific guidelines and minimize confusion. If your child's father is erratic, custody orders can curtail his ability to just "parent at his convenience" because there will be set visitation dates and times that will be designated as his "parenting time." If your child's father is absent or a deadbeat, custody orders that identify you as the parent with sole legal and physical custody will ensure that there is no misunderstanding regarding who has custody and control of your child in the event that your child's father suddenly decides to show up unexpectedly demanding immediate access to your child. Having an established order will also decrease the difficulty in challenging any claims that you are keeping your child from their father, interfering with his parental rights, or other similar allegations. Hopefully you've already secured custody and visitation orders for your children. Nonetheless, it's better late than never, so if you have not, now is a good time to prepare to do so.

Mediation

If you and your child's father are not yet to a point of accord and able to reach an agreement on your own, or if you simply want a professional to facilitate discussion between you two, mediation may be an ideal solution for you rather than jumping to litigation. Because my law practice also includes mediation, I'm able to compare the results of both processes. Although I'm successful achieving favorable results for my clients through litigation (the court trial process) mediation is a far more beneficial option in my opinion. I think mediation is the best way to get the best custody orders for your family because you are able to work with a professional who can help you make knowledgeable decisions, while also working with your co-parent to make sure that those decisions are best for your family.

Mediation is one of the most practical ways for parents to resolve disputes related to child custody, time-sharing, visitation, child support, and co-parenting. As no divided family is the same, no two mediators are the same and no two mediation sessions will be the same. However, typically, mediation takes place in a relaxed, yet structured atmosphere. Parents meet with the mediator to facilitate an open discussion during which they are able to confidentially communicate and discuss any issues of concern, goals, and proposed solutions.

The mediator is a neutral party. Through my mediation process, although I do not represent either party, I work carefully with both parents to help them figure out what will work best for *their* divided/blended family. I will then specifically tailor a unique agreement for the parents, which will ultimately be submitted to the Court with a request that it be made an enforceable court order.

Formal Request for Order

Unfortunately, not all parents will be able to reach an agreement regarding custody/visitation of their children. The last resort, if you and your child's father have been unable to agree on issues related to your child, may be to file a motion or other request for the court to make specific orders related to the custody and support of your child. When you hear people say "I'll see you in court," this is the process they are referencing. This is the least preferred method of handling things the legal way because it can be very risky and daunting for many reasons:

<u>Family Court Child Custody proceedings are lengthy.</u> Compared to mediation, which is typically completed in a few sessions, family law litigation is a much lengthier process. Although temporary orders may be issued shortly after your case begins, getting permanent orders takes time – in some cases, a very long time. Exactly how long depends on you, the other parent, any lawyers that are involved, and how much conflict exists.

<u>When you litigate, no one "wins."</u> There is no such thing as really "winning" in a litigated custody case. Asking the court to make decisions related to your family is risky because you will likely not get 100% of what you want. To get just 1/2 of what you want will likely cost you a lot of time and money required to build the case.

<u>Legal Battles are Expensive</u> even if you don't hire a lawyer to represent you, you may quickly find out that there is no "cheap" way to litigate a case. Filing fees, service of process charges, court reporters, professional evaluations, and more can easily lead to thousands of dollars in costs. And once lawyers get involved on either side, that amount can easily triple.

<u>Judges don't know you.</u> When you litigate your case, you're essentially putting your family's life into the hands of a stranger. They don't know anything about you, your child's other parent,

or your children. Their decision is solely based on what is presented to them as evidence. Quite frankly, we all know that evidence presented to the court is not always the best reflection of the true circumstances or complete facts (especially if you don't have a lawyer).

The best interest of your child The court is going to make a determination based on what it feels is in the "best interest" of YOUR child (who they know nothing about and may never meet). Your definition of "best interest" and the court's idea of best interest may be on two different spectrums. The court's order may not make any sense for your family, but once it's issued, you have to follow it unless you and the other parent can finally agree to change it. If you and your child's other parent can put your differences aside and really think about what's best for your child, you'll probably be much better off.

Judges are human Granted, they are humans with decision power not afforded to the average layperson, but...the fact still remains that, at the end of the day, they are just like you. They have a life, family, things on their "to do" list, and more. So, although it's easy to put them on a pedestal, just like you they make mistakes, have bad days, get frustrated, don't understand, and are at work. Don't walk into the courthouse expecting to appear before a supernatural human that can work magic...you'll be disappointed.

Agreements feel better When you are able to sit down with the other parent and compromise, although you may not get everything you want, you'll at least know that what you're getting will be something that is reasonable based on your family's needs. Agreements open the door to cooperation. It's not something that is forced, but a decision YOU had a hand in.

For this reason, once you're able to reach an agreement on the bigger issues, you'll slowly be able to reach an agreement on other things and learn to work together for the benefit of your child.

The fact of the matter is, when you are asking a court to make a decision that affects your life, they will not always get it right. With that in mind, if at all possible, you should avoid getting to the point that the court has to make a decision that could change your family's life (for better or worse) for you.

Parenting Plans:

Regardless of which process used to obtain your formal custody orders, in order for your custody orders to benefit your family, many things must be considered.

There are typically several things that are automatically included. Things such as which parent will have the custody and control of the children during each day, who will be in charge of specific extracurricular activities, where the children will go to school, who the children will be with during the holidays, who the medical providers will be, rules required to change the child's school etc. are generally included in most plans.

However, there are several things that oftentimes go unmentioned that you may want to consider discussing during your negotiations or requesting in your formal requests submitted to the court. While it's impossible to include every single foreseeable important issue in your parenting plan, the point of a parenting plan/custody orders is to ensure that there is little room for misunderstanding, misinterpretation, and that the plan can easily be enforced if the need arises. Just like any other contract, more is better than less. The more specific and clear you are regarding the terms of the agreement, the less confusion and conflict there will likely be. When developing your parenting plan, there are many things to consider, but the most important thing that should guide you in making decisions, is what's best for your children.

Here are a few specifics to consider including in your parenting agreement:

1. Who is responsible for transporting your children to and/or from one parent to the other? Where will custody exchanges take place and at what time? May 3rd parties be present during the exchanges? (If one parent is often in the company of someone who likes to initiate or instigate conflict, you can ask the court for orders specifying who can and cannot be present during exchanges.

2. What happens if one parent has to cancel their time? Do they get makeup time with your child? Or is it just forfeited?

3. What if one parent decides to move? Do they have to provide the address to the other parent? (they should), and how far in advance or after the move should the new address be provided to the other parent?

4. Child care – who is allowed to babysit your children? Friends? Family? A mutually chosen babysitter? Anyone?

5. Will the children get phone time with the other parent when they aren't with them and vice versa? If so, on what days, how many times? And at what specific time?

6. New significant others – when will they be able to meet your children?

7. Contact with certain people – are there certain people you agree should not have contact with your children?

8. Does either parent have special decision making authority on certain issues? For example: is one parent in charge of selecting sports teams, extracurricular activities, the school the children will attend, etc.? Or must all of these things be decided jointly. What happens if you can't agree on things requiring joint decision? Is there a neutral party who can act as your "tie breaker"? Or do you have a "rock-paper-scissors" type of solution? (Yes, this matters, because otherwise you'll end up in front of a judge over every disagreement.)

9. Who will have your children for which holidays? Where will holiday exchanges take place and at what exact day and time? If you are splitting spring break, are you meeting at 12 noon on the day that marks halfway mark?

10. What is the remedy if either parent habitually violates the agreement? Do you intend for the agreement to be enforced by law enforcement if necessary? If so, specifically state this in the agreement, as some law enforcement agencies are reluctant to get involved if it's not specified.

11. And of course we can't forget provisions related to expenses – who will be financially responsible for childcare/school tuition? Who will cover the costs of

extra-curricular activities? What about medical insurance premiums and uninsured medical expenses, etc.

Although no parenting plan is the same, and all of the above is not necessary for every family, these are just a few of the provisions to consider including in your agreement to avoid confusion and provide clarity, just in case. It's better to have a lot of unnecessary specifics than to not be specific enough, and leave room for mix up.

Been There, Done That- the last resort:

So what happens when you have honestly put in countless effort to develop a peaceful parenting relationship with your child's father, but your efforts have failed? What if your child's father still does not cooperate and deliberately violates a court ordered parenting plan? Sadly, there will be some dads that no matter what you do to develop a positive relationship with him, he will not cooperate and will do (or won't do) whatever he can in order to make your life miserable. There will always be that one who just doesn't care! He doesn't care about his child, you, or even himself for that matter. The good news is that if you have handled your case the legal way, you will have remedies. Although the process that comes with resorting to these remedies is yet again, disruptive and frustrating for you, nonetheless the remedies are available and you are still better off than you would be if you had not handled things the legal way. Once you have a court order in place, you have a few options in the event that your child's father refuses to follow the court order. Below are the two most commonly used:

❖ *Enforcement:*

In the event that your child's father (or you) violates the court order related to child custody, many states will enable law enforcement officers to enforce the order. To do this, you will need to take a certified copy of your court order to the nearest police station and file a report. You may request that an officer enforce the order. If the department is willing to enforce the order, they will go to the location where your child is being withheld and speak to the parent in violation of the order and demand that they turn over the child. If he follows the officer's request, the officer will then bring your child to you. In the event that your child's father refuses to turn your child over, in some cases the officer will make an arrest, but in most, the officer will usually make a police report so that you may file a court action for enforcement/contempt.

❖ *Contempt:*

A contempt action may be filed if you or child's father willfully violates the child custody, child support, or any other court order. Contempt actions are criminal in nature and for the most part are considered misdemeanors, punishable by up to six months in county jail and/or a fine up to $1,000. These are obviously measures that hopefully you will not be forced to make, but as the CEO of your divided family, it is imperative that you know of your rights and duties as a parent, and be ready and willing to utilize all options available to ensure the welfare and safety of your child.

V.

THE BUSINESS OF

CO-PARENTING

The business of co-parenting is just like any other business; it takes genuine commitment, hard work, and constant, conscious efforts. Although it may require major adjustments in the way you have been dealing with your divided family, once you take full responsibility for your mindset and your actions, and can keep them in check regardless of what your child's father is doing, you will become a master of you and your child's future and your ability to live in peace.

Just like businesses have bylaws to abide by, so should your blended family. There are several things that if implemented, can prevent, lessen, and even destroy drama in your family. Although all divided/blended families are different, the general co-parenting "business" rules can be applied to all and expanded upon as you see fit.

Co-parent business bylaws

❖ *Blended Family Language*

As divided/blended families, we already face an uphill battle to get to a point that we feel like a solid family unit. The way you speak of your family is just one of the things that impacts the dynamic of your

118

relationship. One of the ways to think about it, when someone's words are encouraging, we feel good. When someone speaks well of us, it makes us happy. The same goes for your family. If you speak of your family as though you are unified, at some point you will likely be. If you speak of your family like you're divided, that's how you'll remain if you don't.

"Baby Mommas and Baby Daddies"

Naturally, you may refer to your child's father as your "ex", or worse- your "baby daddy." Unless your family is on a drama filled reality TV show (or unless that's your goal), you should stop referring to your child's father as your "baby daddy." When I looked up the definition of the word "baby daddy," I was baffled by the results. First off, it was nearly impossible to find a definition in the Merriam Webster Dictionary. So, my only resort was to refer to the "urban" and "slang" dictionaries available online. Secondly, the majority of the definitions revealed, were different variations of something like this:

"The father of a woman's child, especially of a child born out of wedlock, but is no longer involved with the mother of the child/children, and more than likely not supporting the children."

Now, you may feel that this definition is accurate, and it may very well be at this very moment. But, is this the reality you desire?

Believe it or not, we speak our worlds into existence. If all you want is a "baby daddy," then carry on referring to him as such. However, if it's your desire to have a positive father figure in your child's life, you should start speaking that over him. That is your child's father, your co-parenting partner. You are your child's mother. Respect and refer to each other as such.

"The Steps"

Yes, we know that a "stepfamily" is one in which one or both spouses have children from another relationship. But, when families blend, why is there a need to distinguish? Everyone in the family knows who the "mom", "dad", and "step"-parents are, there's really no need to remind each other every day. To me, referring to your family as a "step" anything only adds an element of separation. The only time I refer to my stepson as my "stepson" is if I'm providing a detailed explanation that requires it (such as this book). When I introduce him to someone, I refer to him as my son. When I speak of him, I always say "I have three children", not "I have two of my own and one stepchild." We are one family unit, regardless of our bloodline, and there's no reason for us to feel otherwise.

It was no different for my ~~step~~son. Before we decided that "step" was just not a word we would use in our family, I could see the discomfort in his demeanor when he would introduce or refer to me as his "stepmom." Now, he comfortably refers to me as his mom (and clarifies if necessary), bonus mom, or mom #2. This decreases the need for him to provide an explanation about our relationship to those who don't really need it.

If you have to distinguish between your biological and marital relationship, try using "bonus child" "bonus mom" or "bonus dad" instead of "step." Step feels more like a burden or inconvenience, while "bonus" feels more like an advantage, something special, something more solid.

Disparaging remarks

Again, the words you speak regarding your divided/blended family are instrumental in the dynamic of your relationships. This includes not only the words you use to refer to your family members, but also the words you use to describe them. The mantra "If you don't have anything nice to say, don't say anything at all" is best applied here.

Disparaging remarks are those words that are derogatory, disapproving, or critical. You know, the ones you may speak (or be tempted to speak) on you and your child's father's worst day. The words you want to say about him, but you shouldn't say out loud. The words that if your child were to hear them, would make them uncomfortable. Think about it like this: Regardless of how you feel about your child's father, the fact remains that he is still their dad. He is *your* Ex, but not your child's ex. Your relationship with him may be over, but his relationship with his child will remain forever. Considering this, it's imperative that you not be the cause of any dysfunction in their relationship. By making negative comments about your child's father to them, in their presence, or within their hearing distance, you can potentially cause them to feel negatively about their father. You in essence may be transferring your own personal emotions and opinions to them. The same goes for your friends and family; their negative opinions about your child's father are off limits in the presence of your children. Children repeat what they hear grown-ups say, they learn what we teach them. What are you teaching them about their father? Your negative perceptions of him may be correct. However, it's not your job to ruin their independent perception of him. The reality is, if he's really as "bad" as you think, you won't have to say one word to your child about it; he/she will learn everything they need to know about him on their own, based on his actions and interactions with them.

❖ *Check your Village*

Ever heard the quote: "It takes a village to raise a child?" This quote speaks volumes. In order for children to thrive and develop into the wonderful human beings they have the potential to become, they need positive, supportive, influential people in their lives to give them direction and teach them core values of life. The same applies to your co-parenting relationship with your child's father. In order to get to a place of peace and cooperation with your child's father, you must be surrounded by people who support this goal. There's nothing worse than someone who has good intentions when it comes to doing something positive, yet is surrounded by naysayers and people with negative attitudes whose energy transfers to them.

I remember there was a lady who followed me on social media and was interested in one of my resources/programs for divided/blended families. She tagged her friend in the comments of one of my promotional posts indicating that she was thinking of participating in my program because she was tired of the drama with her child's father. Rather than supporting her, her "friend" responded in the comments, basically saying "you don't need this, you do just fine being both mom and dad for your child." This was so disappointing to me: here you had a young lady who acknowledged the fact that she was struggling to build a positive relationship with her child's father and was considering getting help to change her situation. Yet, the one friend that she may have called on for sound advice basically told her "you don't need to change anything, your child is just fine without their dad." This is the perfect example of needing to check your village.

Ever heard the saying "show me who your closest friends are and I'll show you your future"? Yet another mantra that applies to divided/blended families. If your circle consists of a bunch of single, bitter, "baby mamas" whose children don't have relationships with their dads, naturally you may take on the same attitude.

However, if you're surrounded by single moms who are constantly on a mission to create better for their children, then you will naturally be inspired to strive for the same. It's hard to aim for progress when no one around you is progressing. It's hard to be optimistic about your partnership with your child's father if everyone around you is negative. It's hard to build a life of greatness for your child, if everyone around you is content with mediocrity. So, take a moment, think about the top five people who you call on regularly for friendship and really think about the kind of energy they give out. Are they shining light into your life? Or are they more often consumed with darkness. If you want to change your situations, you have to check your village, and adjust as necessary.

❖ *The 5 C's of Co-Parenting:*

1) Communication;

2) Compromise;

3) Conflict Prevention;

4) Consideration; and

5) Cooperation.

Communication

Communication is one of the most important aspects of ANY relationship. But it is specifically important when co-parenting. Even if you may believe that certain things are common sense and you should not have to *literally* communicate those things, in reality it is in the best interest of all parties involved that you clearly communicate your thoughts whenever possible. No two people think alike. For example, just because it makes sense to me that my four-year-old should not be allowed to play outside around the neighborhood without adult supervision, does not mean that others believe the same. In fact, I have a neighbor whose two and three-year-old children run all around the neighborhood by themselves. Again, just because it makes sense to *me* that smoking in the presence of your children is not only inappropriate, but also a health risk, I have met people who smoke around their children on a daily basis and do not give it a second thought.

The point is, it is not reasonable to assume that others think and do exactly as you. Nor can you always expect people to know your expectations. We cannot read minds (although some claim to have this power). If you want someone to know something, you have to communicate that something - even if you believe they should know without you telling them. It is better to communicate too much (effectively) than too little. Now, the subject of how to effectively communicate is literally a completely independent topic for another book. However, here are some very basic tips to keep in mind when communicating with your child's father:

1) <u>Remain cool, calm, collected, and respectful-</u> Keep your emotions out of it. If you are angry, upset, frustrated, or just annoyed with him, try to wait until you have cooled off. Once you have cooled off, think of a tactful way to communicate your position to him. Talk *to* him, not *down* to him. Having a condescending tone will only make matters worse. Regardless of how you feel, disrespect is a no-no. No yelling, no profanity allowed. A good approach is to follow the motto "If you don't have anything nice to say, don't say anything at all." While it's okay and oftentimes necessary to explain your position, whether it be agreement or disagreement, you must always do so respectfully.

2) <u>Be clear -</u> Say what you mean, mean what you say. As previously mentioned, we aren't mind readers. Never assume that your child's father "knows" what

you want or need from him and that you are on the same page. You need to be clear in your expectations and make sure that he understands them.

3) <u>Have Co-Parent Meetings:</u> The purpose of these meetings is to discuss issues related to your children only. Essentially, you all sit down at the table, and discuss things that are going well, things that are working, and things that need improvement. Things like progress in school, extracurricular activities, discipline methods, household rules, parenting schedules, planned trips/vacations, and more are on the table and you discuss them in the same way you would at a professional business/company meeting. Have an agenda, take notes, schedule a follow-up meeting, phone conferences, and discuss strategies to ensure that your child thrives.

4) <u>Communicate in writing as much as possible</u> - When it comes to communication related to your child, it's best to communicate in writing as much as possible. If you have an important conversation, send a follow-up email to confirm the conversation to ensure you are on the same page. Not only does this avoid confusion about

what exactly was said, but it also creates a record for you to use in the future if necessary. However, when communicating in writing, try to be mindful of your tone and your choice of words, as unlike verbal communication, you can't take back a text message or email that has been sent.

A great communication tool you may want to consider are 'Our Family Wizard' and 'Talking Parents'. These are both online tools that incorporate calendars and an email-like system that keeps complete records of communications between parents. The good thing about these programs is not only that it helps parents stay organized, but in the event of a dispute, records can be printed out and provided to the court as evidence. The fact that the communication records can be retrieved often serves as an incentive for parents to "play nice" because they know the records may be used against them in court if they've been acting inappropriately.

Compromise

The bottom line is both parents cannot always get what they want when it comes to decisions concerning their child. Therefore, while you may *know* what's best, please remember there are two of you, both parents, whose opinions matter. The best way to prevent potential problems due to disagreement is to understand the importance of compromise. Pick your battles - everything is not worth the fight. Before making a fuss about an issue make sure that you have had ample opportunity to clearly view the full picture. You have to decide what's important to fight over, and what you are willing to compromise on. Carefully consider your child's father's position. Does any of it make sense? Will going with his suggestion hurt your situation? Or are you simply disagreeing because it's not what you had in mind? Insisting that things always go your way, specifically without being reasonable, is not co-parenting and will likely lead to more stress and chaos in the long run.

Conflict Prevention:

I cannot stress enough the importance of being proactive. Discuss issues that may come up later such as religion, education, traveling out of the country, holidays, vacation, when and how to introduce your child to someone you are seriously dating, who is allowed to babysit your child, etc. It's important that you and your child's father establish as many agreements as possible regarding your child while the two of you are on a good note. As mentioned previously, it's even more important that you formalize your agreements and obtain court orders. Another good idea is to put a system in place that will prevent deadlock such as "rock, paper, scissors", drawing out of a hat, flipping a coin, or asking a third, neutral party to make the final decision in the event that you are unable to agree on an issue. This may sound trivial now, but believe me, it may solve problems that are far from trivial when in the heat of the moment.

Consideration

Because there are two parents and one child (or several children), it's important to always have consideration for each other. You must be considerate of each other's time, schedule, feelings, and relationship with your child. Before making major decisions related to your child, discuss them with your child's father so that he can give his input. Before making plans with your child that may interfere with your child's father's custodial time, discuss your proposed plans with him and a possible way to make up that missed time if he wants. Be considerate of his feelings. Unless the two of you just have a close, friendly relationship, do not discuss your personal affairs with your child's father. Discussions about whom you are dating and your love life (outside of that which is relevant to your child) could possibly cause jealousy, or other ill feelings from your child's father and will result in unnecessary tension in your co-parenting relationship.

Always remain considerate of your child's relationship with his or her father. Encourage your child to continue to grow the bond with their father. In spite of how you feel about your child's father, do not say or do things that will make your child uncomfortable about having a relationship with his or her father. Do not make or allow others to make any negative comments to or within the hearing distance of your child, no matter how true they may be. If your child's dad is a deadbeat, it's unnecessary for you to remind your child of this. If your child's father isn't parenting up to your standards, that's not your child's business. That is between you and your child's father. Most importantly, do not argue with your child's father in front of your child. Your disagreements are private matters to be discussed between the two of you. The last thing you need is for your child to develop ill feelings for his or her father due to your comments and actions. This may be very hard to do, but it is crucially important. Always be the bigger person. Trust me, your child will learn what he or she needs to learn about their father on their own, without any input from you. It's better that they learn on their own so that they do not have bitterness towards you in the future.

Cooperation

Co-parenting is all about teamwork. The business of co-parenting will be considerably more successful if you and your child's father support one another. This means that the two of you should attempt to at a minimum have the similar parenting ideals and make sure that your child understands that you are on the same page and are working together for their benefit. If you have an issue with your child, make an effort to incorporate your child's father into your discipline method, even if that just means making a phone call to him in front of your child and informing him about the problem. If for one reason or another your child's father cannot keep his scheduled visitation, help out if you are able to; switch days with him, keep your child an extra day or two, and depend on him to do the same for you.

When it comes to your child's education and extracurricular activities, make sure that you and your child's father are involved as much as possible. Attend parent-teacher conferences and parent council meetings together. When you send correspondence to your child's school, make sure that both of your names are signed on the correspondence whenever practical so that the school is aware that both parents are involved. Cheer your child on together at events. It may seem awkward at first, but you'll get used to it and it will put your child at ease. Remember at the beginning of this book when I said I have personal experience. Trust me, I do. My husband and I have attended parent-teacher conferences with my stepson's mother. As a result, the teacher and other administrators at his school recognized that my stepson has a strong support system. We also attend sports events, award assemblies, and occasionally even birthday parties for my stepson together. Even if we don't sit together the entire time, we acknowledge one another, and interact peacefully. From the outside looking in, you are not able to tell that any ill feelings ever existed between our two homes, and believe me, at one point there was some extreme illness happening. While, initially all of this may have been a bit awkward, ultimately, the benefits outweighed the awkwardness as our divided/blended family has progressed and, as a result, our family lives in peace.

THE BOTTOM LINE

I know the concept of the business of co-parenting may seem like a lot of work. Especially if you have to work hard in an effort to influence your child's father to get on the same page, set aside the drama, and work with you in considering the best interests of your child. But, although it is a process that requires a lot of consideration, strategy, an action on your behalf, tackling the issues discussed in this book and taking action will ultimately pay off. Regardless of what your child's father does or does not do, you and your child deserve to live in peace. This means that in order to achieve this peace, you have to step out of your comfort zone and take control as the CEO of your divided family. Much of the success of your co-parenting relationship depends largely on you. Keep in mind that even the simplest decisions you make may detrimentally affect your child both now and later. The good news is, by making smart, selfless decisions now, your child has a greater chance of having a bright future. And that's the business of co-parenting.

MEET MERISSA V. GRAYSON

Also known as "America's Blended Family Expert," Merissa V. Grayson is a dynamic and driven Lawyer, Author, Mediator and Co-Parenting + Blended Family Advocate.

Merissa's background stems not only from her professional experience as a Child Custody & Family Law Attorney, but also from her experience as a Wife and Stepmother who has personally disentangled the difficult challenges that often come with the territory of divided & blended family living.

Merissa has dedicated her life to helping families around the country tackle similar challenges by truly walking them through positive transformations to help them gain the lifestyle and peace of mind they deserve.